The Only Person in Your Way is You

How to Stop Fighting Your Season and Start Living in Sync

By Anton Cunningham
Published by Kaja Publishing

ISBN: 979-8-9929023-4-1 (Paperback)
ISBN: 979-8-9929023-5-8 (Hardcover)

Table of Contents

Introduction
Welcome to the Season You're Actually In

A note before we begin: you can read this book as spiritual, psychological, or both. Take what fits your story and leave what doesn't. The seasons don't care what you call them—they're already at work in your life.

There were years when, if something in my life could be ruined by bad timing, I would find a way to ruin it. I pushed for hard conversations that needed space. I tried to harvest before anything had rooted. I clung to what was clearly dying as if my grip could bring it back to life. I thought I had a discipline problem or a motivation problem. Underneath, I had a timing problem. I was fighting the seasons of my own life instead of learning how to live with them.

Right now, as you read this, you're in a season. Not just the one outside your window, but the one pulsing through your relationships, your work, your inner world. It shows up in the text you're avoiding, the decision you keep postponing, the change you know is coming but can't quite face. You may feel behind, broken, or confused—but what if the real issue isn't who you are? What if no one ever taught you how to recognize and move with your seasons?

The earth cycles through winters of loss, springs of possibility, summers of intensity, and autumns of letting go. Nature understands that nothing is meant to bloom all the time. Yet most of us try to live our inner life as if it should be permanent summer—always productive, always on, always thriving. We call it hustle. Nature calls it impossible. When life keeps moving in cycles and we keep insisting on straight lines, the result is overwhelm, burnout, and the quiet conclusion that something must be fundamentally wrong with us. It isn't. You're out of sync with your season.

A while ago, I sat in a therapist's office and spilled everything: I was grieving my mother's death, launching a business, and ending a relationship with a woman I loved deeply. Every part of my life was in a different emotional season, and I was sure I was failing all of them.

My therapist listened, then asked: *"What if you're not failing? What if you're just in multiple seasons at once, and no one ever taught you how to navigate that?"*

That question took all the air out of me. I had been trying to force my whole life into one emotional weather pattern: either grief or joy, building or releasing, fighting or surrendering. But life doesn't work that way. Life gives you spring in one relationship and deep winter in another. It hands you a professional summer while your personal life is in autumn. The exhaustion wasn't from the journey—it was from resisting the seasons I was already in.

We are the only species that fight its seasons. The cost of that resistance is heavy: chronic fatigue, anxiety, resentment, and the constant sense that you are late to a life you were actually right on time for.

The Hidden Cost of Fighting Your Season

Here's what happens when you fight your season:

In a winter season—something ending, dying, going dormant—but you keep trying to make it bloom, you waste energy that could go toward rest, reflection, and honest grief. You're trying to grow roses in frozen ground.

In the spring season, new growth emerges, but you're impatient for full bloom, so you pull up your own seedlings to check if they're growing fast enough. You destroy what's trying to emerge by demanding it arrive fully formed.

In a summer season—activity, abundance, harvest—but you can't receive it because you're still staring at last winter's losses, the harvest rots on the vine while you look backward.

In an autumn season—natural endings, necessary release—but you keep trying to hold everything green, you become a careful curator of dead leaves, afraid to let anything fall.

What finally changed my life wasn't another productivity system or mindset trick. It was realizing that most of the places I felt stuck, ashamed, or behind were signs I was fighting the season I was in. I was trying to save relationships in their natural ending season. I was rushing career transitions that needed more time in the soil. I was forcing myself to be "over" grief that had its own sacred timeline. The shift that changes everything is simple: instead of asking "What's wrong with me?" you start asking "What season am I in?"

Your relationship that feels hard might be a winter conversation you're trying to have with spring expectations. Your career that feels stuck might be a field lying fallow, preparing for a planting you can't see yet. You are not behind. You are misreading your timing.

What Is Seasonal Intelligence?

Most self-help quietly promises permanent summer: endless growth, constant positivity, perpetual winning. It tells you how to optimize and outperform yourself into a version of life where hard seasons are glitches you can fix with enough effort. Not only is that unrealistic—it's unnatural.

This book offers something different: Seasonal Intelligence.

Seasonal Intelligence is the ability to read your life's timing accurately, respond to what each season actually needs instead of what you wish it were, and trust the process even when you can't control it. It has three pillars:

- **Read**: Accurately identify which season you're in—for your relationships, your work, your inner life.
- **Respond**: Give each season what it actually needs instead of forcing it to match a different one.
- **Trust**: Hold multiple seasons simultaneously without losing yourself—because that's what real life demands.

You won't learn how to bypass winter, skip autumn, or stretch summer forever. You'll learn to move with each season so you stop wasting strength fighting what you cannot change and start using that strength where it matters.

This is not about loving every moment. It's about understanding what each moment is *for*.

What This Book Will Give You

This is not a quick-fix manual that promises to remove your problems in five easy steps. Your problems are not the main issue. Your relationship with life's timing is.

By the end of this book, you will be someone who:

- Recognizes which emotional season you're in across every major area of life and understands why fighting those seasons drains your energy.
- Stop self-sabotaging by trying to harvest what's not ready, hold onto what needs to die, or rush through transitions that need time to unfold.
- Knows when to push and when to wait, when to speak and when to stay silent, when to fight and when to let go.
- Can hold multiple seasons at once without losing your mind, because that is what real life demands.

This wisdom is ancient. It lives in the patterns of nature, in the poetry of Ecclesiastes, in the stories of people who learned, usually the hard way, what happens when you honor or ignore your seasons. What we call ancient wisdom is really a relay race of lived experiments: millions of ordinary lives discovering what keeps a soul honest, then handing that forward in stories, rituals, and practices.

Your story is part of that river now. The details of your life are unique, but the underlying patterns are not. A grandmother's hard-won boundary becomes a granddaughter's starting point. A mentor's painful lesson about timing becomes an athlete's turning point.

One person's recovery map becomes another person's survival guide. Whenever you receive wisdom and actually live it, you refine it, personalize it, and eventually offer it back into the current.

The Thirteen Seasons — A Quick Reference

Over the next thirteen chapters, you'll move through emotional seasons that echo one of the oldest texts ever written: a time to be born and a time to die, to plant and uproot, to break down and build, to weep and laugh, to mourn and dance, to keep and to let go, to be silent and to speak, to love and to hate, to wage war and to make peace.

Here's the ground we'll cover:

MOVEMENT ONE: FOUNDATIONS

- Season 1 — **A Time to Be Born & A Time to Die**: Honoring endings and beginnings as partners, not enemies.
- Season 2 — **A Time to Plant & A Time to Uproot**: Knowing when to invest deeply and when to release completely.

MOVEMENT TWO: PROTECTION & HEALING

- Season 3 — **A Time to Kill & A Time to Heal**: Ending what is harming you so real recovery can begin.
- Season 4 — **A Time to Break Down & A Time to Build**: The necessary destruction that precedes genuine construction.

MOVEMENT THREE: EMOTIONAL FLUENCY

- Season 5 — **A Time to Weep & A Time to Laugh:** Letting grief and joy coexist without canceling each other out.
- Season 6 — **A Time to Mourn & A Time to Dance**: Moving through loss and celebration without getting stuck in either.
- Season 7 — **A Time to Keep Silent & A Time to Speak:** Using silence and speech as tools, not reflexes.
- Season 8 — **A Time to Tear & A Time to Mend:** Knowing when a relationship needs honest rupture versus patient repair.

MOVEMENT FOUR: RELATIONAL & MORAL WISDOM

- Season 9 — **A Time to Keep Silence & A Time to Speak:** When words serve and when they harm.
- Season 10 — **A Time to Love & A Time to Hate:** Reclaiming hate as righteous clarity, not cruelty.
- Season 11 — **A Time of War & A Time of Peace:** When to stand firm and when to lay down arms.
- Season 12 — **A Time to Embrace & A Time to Refrain:** The wisdom of closeness and distance.

MOVEMENT FIVE: CONVERGENCE

- Season 13 — **A Time for Every Purpose:** Holding all seasons simultaneously with grace.

How to Use This Book

While the chapters build on each other, each season also stands on its own. Read straight through for the full framework or jump to the season that matches what you're living right now. Return to specific seasons as life shifts.

Every chapter includes: a core story that opens the pattern, an explanation of why we get stuck there, two or three high-impact examples, the main shift that unlocks the season, a Season Practice you can do immediately, and a brief "If you only remember one thing..." takeaway to hold onto when life gets loud.

You don't have to master all thirteen seasons at once. You only have to be honest about the one you're in, and willing to learn its language.

Your Invitation

The most peaceful, genuinely fulfilled people aren't the ones who've figured out how to avoid hard seasons. They're the ones who've learned to read the seasons, trust the timing, and respond with what each season actually needs.

Your seasons are not your enemy. They are your teacher, your guide, and your path to becoming who you were made to be.
When you're ready, turn the page. We'll begin with the season that changes everything else: learning when things need to be born—and when they need to die.

MOVEMENT ONE: FOUNDATIONS
Understanding the Basic Rhythms of Change

Everything in this book grows from two rhythms. Not twelve. Not fifty. Two. Under every breakup, career pivot, identity shift, faith crisis, or fresh start, the same two rhythms are quietly pulsing: things are being born and dying, things are being planted and uprooted.

Most of the confusion, shame, and exhaustion you've carried hasn't come from those rhythms themselves; it's come from misreading them or fighting them.

Our culture trains us to treat change like a problem to manage rather than a season to honor. This is not a new confusion. Ecclesiastes named the tension three thousand years ago — not as a problem to be solved, but as a rhythm to be respected. The wisdom was never in controlling the seasons. It was in learning to read them. We're taught to avoid endings at all costs, rush beginnings before we're ready, and never uproot anything we've invested in—because walking away feels like failure. Nature knows better. Seeds require darkness and time. Fields must be cleared before they can be planted. Old growth has to fall so new life can take its place. These rhythms are already in your bones. You've just been taught to distrust them.

Together, these two rhythms don't just explain what's happening in your life right now. They explain why it has always felt this way.

In this first Movement, you'll build the two foundational rhythms that make every other season finally make sense:

The Rhythm of Birth and Death — how endings and beginnings dance together, why every death makes space for a birth, and why trying to have one without the other keeps you stuck and what it costs you to keep living in an expired season.

The Rhythm of Planting and Uprooting — how to know when to invest versus release, why timing matters more than effort, and what happens when you keep watering what's over or refuse to plant what's true and how to tell the difference between patience and avoidance.

When you understand these rhythms, you stop taking so much of life personally. The relationship that's ending is not proof you're defective; it's winter making room for a different spring. The exhaustion you can't explain is not weakness; it's a season calling for rest that you've been refusing to give it. The dream that hasn't sprouted yet is not proof you're behind; it's a seed still doing its underground work.

Let's start where all honest growth begins: not with a strategy, but with courage. The courage to let what needs to die, die — and the courage to let what wants to live, live.

Season One:
A Time to Be Born & A Time to Die

Life has a twisted sense of humor. Just when you think you've finally got things figured out, it hands you a birth certificate and a death certificate on the same day. Not literally—but emotionally, it can feel exactly like that: you get the dream job the same week your marriage falls apart, or you finally stop drinking and realize you've also lost your entire social circle, start therapy the day after your best friend moves across the country, or discover who you really are just as you realize you have to let go of who you thought you were.

Last Tuesday, Marco sat with me at the Egg Harbor cafe, holding two pieces of paper. In his left hand: divorce papers he'd finally signed after two years of trying to save his marriage. In his right: an acceptance letter from the graduate program he'd dreamed about since college. He was sobbing and laughing at the same time, and when he finally tried to explain what he was feeling, all he could manage was: *"How can the worst and best day of my life be the same day?"*

Welcome to the most fundamental truth about being human. Marco wasn't confused. He was experiencing something most of us are never given language for. Birth and death are not opposite experiences that happen separately. They are dance partners, always moving together, each making space for the other.

Right now, something in your life is trying to be born—a new version of yourself, a different way of relating, a dream developing in the dark. And right now, something in your life is trying to die—an outdated identity, a relationship that has run its course, a belief system that no longer serves you.

Your mind wants to deal with these separately: "Let me grieve this first, then I'll celebrate that." Life hands you both at once and says, "Here. Hold them together."

The Pattern That's Making You Exhausted

Here's where you're probably getting in your own way: you're trying to have births without deaths, or deaths without births. You want a new relationship without ending the old patterns that sabotage intimacy.

You want a career change without letting go of the identity you've spent ten years building. You want growth without loss, gain without sacrifice, and resurrection without the part that comes first.

Or maybe you're on the other side. You're so focused on what's dying that you can't see what's trying to be born. So deep in grief about your marriage ending that you can't feel the first quiet stirrings of who you're becoming. So focused on the job you lost that you can't see the parts of you that are finally free to breathe.

Both patterns lead to the same place: exhaustion from fighting life's most basic rhythm. You feel like you're failing—but you're just out of sync with your season.

What you're building in this season is emotional acceptance — not resignation, but the rare ability to acknowledge what is actually happening without immediately trying to fix, reverse, or explain it away. Most people spend years fighting the terms of their own lives. They argue with endings, delay beginnings, and exhaust themselves maintaining a version of reality that has already changed. Emotional acceptance has one job: get honest about what is actually happening, then take the next step. Not happiness. Not certainty. Just honesty and one step forward. It asks you to stop spending your energy on the argument and start spending it on the honest next step. The moment you can look at what is dying and say "yes, this is ending" and look at what is stirring and say "yes, something new is here" — you free up more internal resources than any productivity system ever could.

Your mind thinks it's protecting you. It doesn't realize that sometimes protection becomes prison.

The Death of Who You Used to Be

Let's start with the part most of us avoid: the death of who you used to be. Right now, millions of people are walking around in expired identities, wearing old versions of themselves like clothes that stopped fitting years ago. The former athlete still living off decade-old glory. The divorced person still planning their life around someone who left. The parent whose kids are grown but who doesn't know who they are when there's no one left to take care of.

Your mind is brilliant at keeping you in expired seasons. It says, "You're forty-five, it's too late to start over." It pulls up LinkedIn at midnight to show you how far behind you are. It calculates how many years you've "wasted" if you change direction now. But every identity has an expiration date—not because you failed, but because you grew. The Roman emperor Marcus Aurelius called this 'dying before you die' — the willingness to let one version of yourself expire so a truer one could step forward. The people who do this well don't call it failure. They call it becoming. The person who has got you here isn't the person who will get you there.

Darius was a successful lawyer who had built his entire identity around winning cases and climbing the partnership ladder. At thirty-eight, he had everything his twenty-five-year-old self had dreamed of: a corner office, a six-figure salary, and respect from his colleagues. He also had chronic insomnia, a failing marriage, and a growing sense that he was living someone else's life.

"I can't just throw away twelve years of work," he told me. *"Everyone thinks I'm successful. My parents brag about me. What would I even do instead?"*

Darius was experiencing identity death anxiety—the terror of letting go of who you've been, even when that identity is slowly killing you. His lawyer identity needed to die not because being a lawyer was wrong, but because his reasons for becoming one were built on his father's dreams, not his own.

He didn't quit overnight; that would have been reckless. Instead, he began loosening his grip on his identity while exploring what he wanted to be born. He signed up for a pottery class he'd secretly wanted to try for years. He reduced his caseload. He stopped introducing himself as "Darius the lawyer" and started just being Darius. Today, he runs a ceramics studio and teaches part-time at a law school. That integration only became possible after he let the old identity die.

This is the part no one celebrates. The Stoics had a word for this — *apatheia* — not apathy, but the freedom from clinging, inner tranquility. The ability to release what has already run its course and feel the ground again. We praise the new business, the new relationship, the before-and-after photo—but we rarely honor the quiet funerals that made those beginnings possible.

When Your Heart Knows but Your Mind Resists

Think about the last time you stayed in a relationship, job, or situation longer than you knew you should. Chances are that your heart had already started the mourning process months before you actually left. You'd had that moment alone in your car or in the shower when you whispered, *"This is over"*, even if you immediately took it back.

But your mind kept making lists of pros and cons. "What if this is a mistake? What will people think? What if I never find anything better?" Your mind demanded guarantees. Your heart was offering invitations.

This is where most of us get stuck. We wait to feel ready, for a moment with zero fear, zero doubt, and zero risk. That moment never comes. Readiness is a myth. The desire for certainty before acting is itself the trap. The action creates clarity. Not the other way around. You will never be fully prepared to let go of something familiar, even when it's slowly suffocating you.

The question isn't "Am I ready?" The question is: "Am I willing to take one honest step in the direction my season is already pulling me?"

The Relationship Graveyard and Nursery

Every relationship you've ever had lives somewhere on the birth-death spectrum. Some are ancient artifacts you occasionally dust off with nostalgia. Some are fresh graves you're still bringing flowers to. Some are newborns you're afraid to hold too tightly. And some are with yourself — the fragile new belief that you might actually be enough.

Right now, some of your relationships are being born, maybe a friendship that started with shared eyerolls in a meeting and is quietly becoming one of the most honest connections you've ever had. Some are dying, that romance where you both keep pretending you're in love when you're really very expensive roommates who argue about the trash.

And some are transforming. Your marriage might be ending, but your co-parenting partnership might finally be taking its first honest breath. Your romance might be flatlining, but a real friendship might be emerging from the ashes.

Kendra and Bree had been best friends for twenty years, inside jokes, shared history, each other's emergency contact. Over time, their paths diverged sharply. Kendra wanted depth, honesty, and growth. Bree wanted gossip, drama, and the surface. Every time they hung out, Kendra left feeling smaller and more exhausted.

"I can't just throw away twenty years," Kendra told me. *"She knows everything about me."*

But the friendship, in its current form, was poisoning her growth. So, she did something most people never do: she stopped performing CPR on it. She quit forcing deep talks with someone who didn't want them. She stopped initiating. She declined invitations that pulled her back into old patterns.

Over six months, the old version of the friendship died. Kendra grieved the shared history, the version of herself that had belonged there. But in that death, something cleaner emerged. Now they see each other a couple of times a year—real but boundaried conversations. The toxic friendship had to die so a smaller, healthier connection could live.

That's the paradox: death makes space for a birth you could not have imagined while you were still clinging to what was.

The Thoughts That Need to Die So New Ones Can Live

It's not just external relationships that go through birth-death cycles. It's the relationship you have with your own thoughts, the stories you tell yourself about who you are and what you're allowed to want. That voice that says you're not good enough. It needs to die. Not because you should never have self-doubt—healthy self-reflection matters—but because that particular voice isn't helping you grow. It's keeping you small. The narrative that you're "always the one who gets left," "always the one who messes it up," "always the one who has to be strong"—those aren't harmless phrases. They are gravestones you keep kneeling in front of.

And those thoughts don't live in isolation. "I'm not good enough" becomes overworking, overexplaining, overpreparing. "My needs are a burden" becomes never asking for help. My needs are a burden that becomes never asking for help. I must control everything, or it falls apart, becomes exhaustion dressed up as responsibility. "If I let myself feel this, I'll fall apart" becomes numbing out with scrolling, food, or endless busyness.

Here's the challenge no one warns you about: these thoughts don't die quietly. They go out kicking and screaming, whispering: "But what if you actually aren't good enough? What if believing in yourself is just setting you up for a fall?" They're familiar. There's a strange comfort in their toxicity; at least you know what to expect.

Seasonal Intelligence is what helps you manage this internal turnover. Instead of treating every emotion like an emergency, you start to ask: "Is this reaction coming from an old season that needs to die, or from the new one that's trying to be born? Is this habit serving the season I'm in right now, or is it leftover equipment from a season I've already outgrown?"

Your emotional management stops being about repression or indulgence and becomes about discernment. Some feelings need expression. Some thoughts need challenging. Some habits need patience. Some patterns need a funeral.

The Grief No One Talks About

There's a kind of grief we rarely name: grieving the death of your problems.

That anxiety that's been your constant companion for fifteen years, the racing heart, the sweaty palms, the 3 a.m. catastrophizing, has made your life miserable and also feels terrifyingly familiar. It has been your excuse for not taking risks, your explanation for why things don't work out. When you start to heal and that anxiety begins to loosen its grip, there's a strange emptiness. Who are you if you're not "the anxious one"? The same thing happens when you outgrow relationships that ran on chaos. Or when you stop being the one who fixes everyone else and realize you don't know what to do with your hands.

Epictetus, who was born into slavery and built a philosophy from it, put it plainly: 'First, say to yourself what you would be; and then do what you have to do.' The invitation is there. The fear is real. Both are true.

The same thing happens when you outgrow relationships that ran on chaos. You might find yourself missing the drama even though you know it was wrecking you. We all have our moments; this is what it means to be human. Beautiful, contradictory, and absolutely real.

The One Blocking Your Path

Remember: the only person in your way is you—but not in the shameful, "you're the problem" way you've been taught. The "you" in your way is not your heart, your intuition, your deepest self. It's the well-meaning part of your mind that is trying to protect you from the very changes you were born to live through.

Your mind is like an overprotective parent who doesn't want you to get hurt. It tells you to stay where it's familiar. It tries to talk you out of everything that involves risk: ending the relationship, starting the business, setting the boundary, and telling the truth. But staying stuck is also a risk. Refusing to let things die when they need to die is a risk. Refusing to let things be born when they're ready is a risk. The cost of your self-protection is often your self-respect.

The mind and fear have always been roommates — one generates the threat, the other calculates the exit. The heart operates on a different frequency entirely. It doesn't calculate. It knows.

Your heart already knows what needs to be born and what needs to die. Your body has been giving you signals—the pit in your stomach when you think about staying, the lightness in your chest when you imagine leaving, the way certain conversations energize you while others drain you completely. Your mind just needs to get out of the way long enough for the natural process to happen.

Every ending creates space for a beginning you couldn't have imagined while you were still clinging to what was. And every beginning eventually gives meaning to the death that made it possible. They are not enemies. They are partners in the rhythm of a life fully lived. This is not a new idea. Ecclesiastes named it three thousand years ago: 'To everything there is a season.' Not a metaphor. A law.

If you only remember one thing from this season, You are not behind. You are being invited to stop fighting the natural rhythm of birth and death and start moving with it. The only person in your way is the part of you that still believes you're safer in an expired season than in an honest one.

Season Practice: Birth and Death Assessment

Name Your Season

Take five minutes. List three things in your life that are trying to be born and three that are trying to die. Don't overthink—write what comes immediately to mind.

Trying to Be Born:

1.

____

2.

____

3.

____

Trying to Die:

1.

____

2.

____

3.

____

Notice Your Mind

Write down the exact sentences your mind uses to resist these births and deaths.

- About what's trying to be born:

  ____

- About what's trying to die:

  ____

Notice Your Body

You don't have to have words for it yet. The body speaks first.

Close your eyes. Think about what needs to die in your life. Where do you feel it—chest, throat, stomach, jaw? Now think about what's trying to be born. Where does that live in your body? Your body often knows the truth before your mind is ready to accept it.

One Aligned Action This Week

Choose one small action that either supports what's trying to be born or allows what's trying to die to actually go.

If supporting a birth: schedule the class, make the phone call, write the first page, send the message.

If allowing a death: stop one life-support behavior, decline one obligation, have one honest conversation.

Threshold Questions: Crossing Into What's Next

What is your mind's strongest argument for keeping what needs to die? What would it cost you to stop listening to that argument?

What is one thing that's trying to be born that you've been too afraid to name out loud? What would it mean to say it clearly—even just to yourself?

Season Summary

- Birth and death are dance partners—each makes space for the other.
- Identity death anxiety is real, and it's not proof you're making the wrong choice.
- You are not broken for grieving and celebrating at the same time. You're sophisticated.
- Readiness is a myth. One honest step is enough.
- The only person in your way is the part of you that still thinks an expired season is safer than an honest one.

Season Two:
A Time to Plant & A Time to Uproot

Where in your life are you still watering something you secretly know will never bear the fruit you hoped for? And where are you standing on bare ground, longing to plant something true, while telling yourself it's safer to leave the soil empty than to risk another beginning? Or maybe the ground has been empty so long it feels safer that way — at least empty ground can't disappoint you.

What relationship, role, belief, or identity are you keeping simply because it has roots—not because it's still alive? What dream or calling are you postponing because real planting would mean slow work, uncertainty, and no guarantee of applause? These aren't abstract questions. They're the fault lines between the life you're maintaining and the life that wants to grow.

Nature moves through this tension every single year without confusion. Fields are cleared. Old stalks are turned back into the soil. Dead branches are cut away to make room for new growth. No farmer expects a harvest from unturned ground or demands instant crops from a seed planted yesterday. The earth understands that uprooting and planting are not enemies; they are partners in the same cycle.

Humans, especially now, struggle with both sides of that cycle. We resist uprooting because we've been taught that longevity equals value. If you've been in a job, a relationship, a city, or a persona for years, walking away feels like betrayal rather than wisdom. At the same time, we resist true planting because we've been trained by instant results—thirty-day transformations, overnight success, life hacks. We want a garden-level harvest on microwave timing. Or we spend years researching the perfect seed, the perfect season, the perfect conditions — and call that gardening.

So, we end up trapped in a double bind. We won't pull up what's overgrown, so our inner soil is crowded and depleted. We won't plant what's real, so our future stays hypothetical.

We pour effort into maintaining what once made sense but no longer fits, and we sprinkle half-hearted seeds on the surface of our real desires, then call it "trying" when nothing grows.

This season is about breaking that pattern.

The Pattern That's Destroying Your Energy

You're exhausted because you're trying to keep everything alive, every relationship, every opportunity, every version of yourself you've ever been.

Your life has started to resemble one of those yards where nothing is ever removed, only added. At first, it looks full and lush; eventually, it becomes crowded and chaotic. Nothing has space to thrive because everything is fighting for the same limited resources: your time, your attention, your nervous system.

Or maybe you're on the other end of the spectrum. You're so afraid of commitment that you uproot everything the moment it requires real work. You leave relationships at the first sign of conflict. You abandon projects when the honeymoon phase ends. You pull up dreams the second they don't bloom on schedule.

Both patterns lead to the same wasteland: a life where nothing ever fully grows because you don't know the difference between what needs patient cultivation and what needs decisive removal.

Seasonal Intelligence begins when you can look at your life and say honestly: "Something is staying only because it has roots, not because it still has life."

The Field That Had to Be Ruined First

In a small rice village in Japan, an old farmer taught his grandson the real meaning of planting and uprooting. He didn't start with a lecture— he handed the boy a hoe and led him into the flooded paddies.

Before a single seedling could be transplanted, they pulled up last year's dead stalks, tore out stubborn weeds, leveled the soil, and broke apart clumps that had hardened over winter. To the boy, it looked like they were ruining the field. To his grandfather, they were making it ready.

Later, the grandson understood that the lesson hadn't just been about rice. The richest seasons of his life grew out of ground he'd had the courage to disturb. What felt like loss or destruction was often quiet preparation—and clearing what no longer belonged was itself an act of creation.

Long before anyone had language for "mindset" or "self-work," farmers already understood what most of us still resist: you can't keep every plant just because you worked hard to grow it. The Talmud teaches that every blade of grass has its angel bending over it, whispering 'Grow.' But the angel can't work in soil that has never been turned.

Ancient agrarian laws required fields to rest, and corners of the harvest to be left unclaimed, a built-in reminder that not everything must be maximized, and not everything should be kept. Real abundance comes from the courage to disturb the soil, pull up what's finished, and trust that empty ground is not waste. It's preparation.

Most of us want the harvest without the muddy middle. But there is no genuine planting without honest uprooting.

What You're Still Watering That Stopped Growing

Every relationship in your life is somewhere on the planting-uprooting spectrum. Some are perennials, returning stronger after each winter. Some are annuals, beautiful for a season and then complete. Some are weeds, arriving uninvited, spreading fast, choking out everything else.

That friend who only calls when they need something is a weed masquerading as a flower. You keep watering it because it's familiar and because pulling it feels unkind. But every day you leave it in the ground, it steals nutrients from relationships that could actually thrive.

That romantic relationship you're trying to resurrect isn't a plant anymore—it's a root system from something that was once beautiful but is now just taking up space. Uprooting it doesn't mean it was never valuable. It means its season is over.

The scariest part of uprooting isn't the loss. It's the empty space left behind—the silence where drama used to live, the free time where chaos used to fill your schedule. That emptiness forces the question you've been avoiding: "What do I actually want to plant here?"

That question is where your real life begins. That includes the relationship with the version of yourself you've been trying to keep on life support.

The Plants That Require Sacrifice

In emotional gardening, the most meaningful things require the most to grow.

You cannot plant a dream career in soil still occupied by your fear of failure. You cannot grow authentic self-respect in ground crowded with toxic self-talk. You cannot cultivate a healthy relationship in a heart still trying to resurrect a dead one.

Some plants, the ones that will actually sustain you, require you to uproot not just the obvious weeds but also some "good" things that are simply in the way. When you decide to plant a new calling or a new way of living, you quickly discover your life is already full. To make room, you must dig up the reflexive yes to every invitation that drains you. You have to pull up the habit of numbing out instead of nurturing what matters. You must dig out the belief that your dreams are selfish.

None of those things are inherently evil. Time with friends is good. Helping others is beautiful. But when they occupy the exact space where your dream needs to grow, something has to move. Sometimes, the thing in the way isn't a commitment or a relationship; it's the version of yourself that prefers not knowing over the risk of trying.

The hardest part of this season isn't pulling the obvious weeds. It's recognizing that some perfectly good things must be sacrificed so the one thing you truly want can flourish.

The Underground Work Nobody Sees

The shiny "follow your dreams" posts never talk about the underground work. Every visible breakthrough you've ever admired had months of invisible work underneath it that nobody photographed. Most of planting and uprooting happens where no one can see it, celebrate it, or post about it.

When you finally have the conversation where you end a toxic relationship, that's not the hard part—that's the moment something that has been dying underground for months finally breaks the surface. The real work was the quiet decision to stop responding to every crisis. The gradual withdrawal of your emotional energy from their drama. The slow rediscovery of who you are when you're not constantly managing someone else's feelings. Those were the nights you were loosening roots, one boundary at a time.

The same is true with planting. The day you quit your job to start your own business is not when the work begins—it's when all the underground preparation becomes visible. The real planting happened in the research, the savings, the skill-building, and the terrifying shift from "Who am I to do this?" to "Who am I not to at least try?"

Roots develop long before anything breaks the surface. Your job in this season is to respect the root phase instead of calling it "nothing happening."

The Achievement Trap

Logan called what he had achievement addiction.

He was a successful surgeon, published researcher, and marathoner. Every achievement was barely celebrated before it was replaced by the next goal. *"I literally can't stop,"* he said. *"If I'm not achieving something, I feel like I'm dying."*

Logan's mental garden was full of thoughts planted in childhood: "You're only valuable when you're producing." "Rest is laziness." "Worth equals achievement." These weren't just thoughts—they were massive root systems wrapped around everything he was.

Uprooting them felt like betraying his immigrant parents, who had sacrificed everything for his success. It felt like killing the very thing that had made him. But those beliefs were choking out everything else—joy, relationships, health, peace. They were weeds disguised as prize roses.

He didn't rip them out overnight. There were weeks before he felt like a traitor to everyone who had believed in the old version of him. He slowly loosened their grip while planting new thoughts alongside them: "I have inherent worth." "Rest is productive." "Success includes happiness."

At first, the new beliefs felt fake—fragile seedlings in soil dominated by the old patterns. But with daily practice, therapy, and deliberate attention, they grew strong enough to crowd out what had been there before. Logan still achieves. The difference is that now he does it of his own choice, not by compulsion. The toxic roots had to be fully uprooted for the healthier ones to take hold. That's the quiet, holy work of this season.

Replanting the Mind

The most important planting and uprooting you'll do happens in the garden of your own mind.

Some thoughts you've nurtured for years produce genuine fruit. Others choke out everything else, trying to grow. The reflex to always expect the worst may have protected you once—now it keeps you too exhausted to plant anything that requires hope. The belief that you must earn love by being perfect has roots deeper than you think. It wires how you receive feedback, which relationships you tolerate, how you handle success, and how you talk to yourself when you make mistakes. You can't snip that belief at the surface. You have to dig out the whole system.

Here's the key: nature hates a vacuum. If you uproot old thoughts without planting new ones, the old ones grow back stronger. Pull weeds without planting grass and you just invite more weeds.

So, when you uproot "I'm not good enough," you must plant something in its place: "I am learning and growing every day." When you pull up "I can't trust anyone," you plant "I can learn to trust wisely." When you dig up "I don't deserve happiness," you sow "I am worthy of love and joy."

At first, these new thoughts feel awkward, seeds in soil that doesn't believe them yet. They need repetition, protection, and deliberate tending. But if you keep at it, they will eventually outgrow the old patterns. And your mind—the one that's been clinging to the weeds, thinking it was keeping you safe—will slowly learn that it doesn't have to protect you from your own growth.

A mind that mistakes familiarity for safety will keep you tending to a dead garden your whole life.

The Art of Knowing What to Keep and What to Pull

The hardest part of this season isn't the act of planting or uprooting. It's the wisdom to know which is which.

When is something worth fighting for, and when is it time to let go? When do you need more patience with something growing slowly, and when do you need to admit it will never thrive in this soil?

We stay in relationships that stopped growing years ago because we remember how beautiful they once were. We abandon dreams that only needed more time because they didn't bloom on our schedule. We plant new habits in the same emotional climate that killed the old ones and wonder why nothing changes.

Learning to plant and uproot well starts with one uncomfortable habit: telling yourself the truth about what you actually feel, not what you think you should feel.

You start noticing what you feel in certain environments instead of what you tell yourself you're supposed to feel. You catch the moment your body tightens when you say yes, the way your energy crashes after certain conversations, the quiet relief you feel when plans fall through. You begin to read these signals not as overreactions but as information. Little by little, you stop judging yourself for having these responses and start using them to decide where to keep investing—and where it's time to gently pull your roots up.

Ask yourself honestly:

- That career you've been trying to make work for five years: are there small signs of real growth, or just more effort with no fruit?
- That friendship that always leaves you drained: do you feel more like yourself after time together, or less?
- That relationship you keep trying to resurrect: are you building something new, or clinging to a memory that no longer exists?
- That story you keep talking about why you can't: is it still true, or is it just well-rehearsed?

Sometimes the weed is not the other person or the job. It's your own avoidance, fear, or insistence on keeping everything exactly as it is. Uprooting means facing emptiness. Planting means investing in what might fail. Your mind will give you a thousand reasons to avoid both. But your heart already knows which parts of your life are quietly asking to be released—and which are begging for a real chance to grow.

The Hidden Harvest

When you learn to plant and uproot on purpose, your life stops feeling like something that happens to you and starts feeling like something you're cultivating.

You begin to recognize when a relationship is ready for deeper investment and when it needs release. You sense when a dream needs more time and when it's time to trade it for a truer one. You identify which beliefs nourish you and which starve you.

You stop asking for permission to remove what is harming you. The Japanese concept of "satoyama" — the landscape between mountain and flat land — describes the most fertile ground as the place in between. Neither fully wild nor fully tamed. That's where you're learning to live. You stop apologizing for planting what other people don't understand. You begin to see planting and uprooting not as signs of instability, but as acts of love—for your present self, your future self, and everyone who benefits from the most alive version of you.

Your garden will never be finished. Weeds will return. Healthy plants will need pruning. That is not failure, that's the ongoing work of a life you've decided is worth tending.

What you're building in this season is emotional discernment — the capacity to distinguish between love that is keeping something alive, and fear that is keeping something on life support. Discernment is one of the least glamorous emotional skills because it asks you to sit in uncertainty long enough to feel the difference between genuine life and stubborn habits. Your feelings are data here: the chronic heaviness you feel in a relationship that should feel nourishing, the persistent quiet excitement about a dream you keep dismissing, the relief that flickers through you when you imagine letting something go. Learning to read those signals accurately — rather than overriding them with logic, guilt, or other people's opinions — is how you stop gardening out of obligation and start gardening out of wisdom.

If you only remember one thing from this season: Not everything with roots deserves to stay. Not every seed deserves to stay in the packet. The only person who decides what grows in your life is you—and you're more capable of that decision than your mind has been willing to admit.

Season Practice: The Garden Assessment

Name Your Season

Take five minutes. List three things that are ready to be planted and three that are ready to be uprooted. Don't overthink—trust your first instinct.

Ready to Plant:

1.

2.

3.

Ready to Uproot:

1.

2.

3.

Notice Your Mind

Write down the exact sentences your mind uses to argue with this list.

- About planting: "You can't because..."

____

- About uprooting: "You shouldn't because..."

____

Seeing these objections on paper helps you recognize they're thoughts, not truth.

Notice Your Body

Put your hand on your chest. Think about what needs uprooting. What physical sensation appears—tightness, heaviness, nausea? Now think about what wants to be planted. Where does that hope live in your body—warmth, expansion, lightness? Your body often tells the truth before your mind is ready to admit it.

One Aligned Action This Week

Choose one small action that either plants or uproots:

If planting: clear one protected hour, buy that book, send that email, sign up for that class.

If uprooting: stop one maintenance behavior, decline one draining invitation, release one obligation that no longer fits.

The Investment Audit

Write down one thing you're maintaining mostly because you've "already put so much into it." Then write what it actually costs you each week in time, energy, or peace. Ask yourself honestly: is the cost worth it in this season?

Root Work: Questions for the Gardener in You

Where are you confusing loyalty with life support? What would it mean to love something enough to let it go?

What is the one thing you most want to plant right now—the thing you keep circling but haven't committed to? What is the real reason you haven't started?

Season Summary

> Your life is a garden—everything in it is either growing, dying, or just taking up space.
> Investment doesn't equal value—time spent doesn't automatically make something worth keeping.
> Empty space is not failure—if you clear it on purpose, you get to choose what fills it.
> Underground work precedes visible change—roots form in darkness before anything breaks the surface.
> Both planting and uprooting are acts of love—removing what doesn't serve you is as sacred as nurturing what does.

You are already gardening, whether you admit it or not. The question isn't whether you're brave enough to do it perfectly. The question is whether you're willing to stop leaving your life on autopilot and start choosing what actually gets to grow.

MOVEMENT TWO: PROTECTION & HEALING
Learning What Must End So You Can Actually Recover

Learning What Must End So You Can Actually Recover

You've started to see the rhythms. Now comes the part nobody warned you about. You've learned that endings and beginnings dance together, that planting and uprooting are part of the same rhythm, and that the structures you live inside were built on blueprints you never fully chose. Now we step into a harder truth: some things in your life aren't just out of season, they are actively harming you. And real healing won't begin until they end.

Almost every wisdom tradition in history has honored endurance. What they rarely taught is the difference between endurance that builds you and endurance that slowly hollows you out. We are taught from an early age that being a good person means being patient, understanding, forgiving, and flexible. So when something hurts, most of us reach for the same tools that earned us approval the first time. We try to out-love the dysfunction, out-explain the misunderstanding, out-work the problem. We stay in relationships, roles, systems, and stories long after our bodies are begging us to leave—because walking away feels like failure, betrayal, or selfishness.

Movement Two is where that script finally meets its match.

There are patterns you cannot heal by being more patient, because the structure itself is harmful. There are roles you cannot redeem by being more selfless, because the role exists to use you. There are beliefs you cannot gently tweak, because they were built on a lie about your worth. In these places, your kindness to others has become cruelty to yourself. And no amount of grace, effort, or good intention will change what the structure is designed to do.

This Movement is where you learn that protection and healing are not soft concepts. They are fierce, clear, and sometimes look like destruction from the outside. The work here asks for something rarer than toughness: the honesty to name what is happening without softening it into something more comfortable. Honest enough to stop performing recovery while the wound is still open. Honest enough to stop calling slow erosion by kinder names. Honest enough to say: 'This cannot be fixed by me trying harder. This needs to end.'

In the chapters ahead, you will learn why ending certain patterns and relationships is a necessary act of love—not a failure of grace. You'll see how real healing requires more than feeling better; it requires changing the conditions that created the wound in the first place. You'll discover why your nervous system keeps pulling you back toward the familiar, even when the familiar is harmful. And you'll begin building a life where your safety, your dignity, and your emotional sanity are non-negotiables—not optional extras you earn by suffering enough first.

You'll meet people who have had to make difficult cuts in their own lives. A son who finally stepped back from an abusive parent and watched his panic attacks stop. A surgeon who helped me understand that cutting out what's toxic and tending what can heal are both acts of love. A surgeon friend that said something over coffee one morning that I haven't been able to unhear. A woman who had to dismantle the beautiful, unlivable life she'd built on someone else's blueprint before she could build one that fit. Their stories will show you that sometimes healing looks less like a spa day and more like a demolition site—and that the demolition is entirely in service of something better.

If Movement One asked, "What season am I in?", Movement Two asks "What here actually deserves to survive?"

The Talmud teaches that preserving one life is equivalent to preserving an entire world. Your life counts in that equation. Protecting it is not selfishness. It is the precondition for everything else you want to give.

You are not obligated to keep participating in what harms you—even if you were raised to believe you are. You are allowed to protect yourself without apologizing. You are allowed to end what must end so that what is genuinely capable of healing can finally begin.

The distinction between what needs to be ended and what needs to be tended — you'll carry that clearly by the time you leave this Movement. And it will change how you see almost every relationship and role in your life. You'll have the language and the inner permission to say *"no more"* in the places where you've been saying "I'll try harder." And you'll begin to understand that your protection and your healing are not selfish—they are the way you become someone who can love from wholeness instead of from wounds.

Season Three:
A Time to Kill & A Time to Heal

There are seasons when being a good person is not enough to move your life forward. You have already been kind, patient, understanding, and reasonable. You've explained yourself a hundred different ways, given second chances and third ones and tenth ones, tried to out-love the dysfunction, outwork the problem, outlast the pain—and still nothing moves in the direction of health. Sometimes the thing that must end isn't a person or a job — it's the version of you that keeps agreeing to be treated that way. That is when this season arrives, not as a gentle suggestion but as a fierce, quiet knowing: something needs to end here, or it will eat everything else.

This is the season where healing begins not with tender care but with clear endings. Endings to patterns, agreements, roles, and systems that cannot be made safe, no matter how tenderly you treat them. It is the uncomfortable recognition that you cannot stitch new life onto structures that were never designed to hold it.

Jared, a surgeon friend of mine, said it plainly over coffee one morning when I was agonizing over ending a toxic friendship. *"It feels so violent,"* I told him, *"Cutting someone out of my life."*

"That's exactly what you're doing," he said. *"And that's exactly what needs to happen."* Then he described his day. *"Today I cut a tumor out of someone's body—violent, precise, necessary. The tumor wasn't evil; it was just growing in the wrong place, stealing resources from healthy tissue. Without removal, it would have killed my patient."* He paused. *"But cutting out the tumor isn't the end. That's just the killing part. The healing part comes after: helping healthy tissue regenerate, preventing infection, and supporting recovery. Both parts are necessary. Both are love."*

That's when something landed for me. Ending toxic patterns and relationships isn't cruelty. It's surgery. The apparent violence serves restoration. The killing makes space for the healing. Most of us were never permitted to think this way. We were handed patience and told it was the same thing as wisdom.

The Confusion Between Harm and Help

Most of us were raised on some version of "If you just try harder, it will get better." Try harder in the relationship. Try harder at the job. Try harder with the family. We were taught that walking away is failure, changing course is quitting, and saying "enough" is selfish or unloving.

So, we stay. We explain. We accommodate. We let our boundaries erode and call it loyalty, maturity, grace. And inside, we quietly die. The Akan people of West Africa have a saying: 'The ruin of a nation begins in the homes of its people.' What quietly destroys you doesn't stay quiet forever — it eventually shapes everything around you.

Here's what nobody says clearly enough: there are dynamics you cannot heal by being more patient, because the structure itself is harmful. There are roles you cannot redeem by being more selfless, because the role exists to use you. There are beliefs you cannot gently tweak, because they were built on a lie about your worth. In these places, staying is not noble. It is destructive.

Part of the work in this season is learning to trust what your body has been trying to tell you for a long time. The way your breath goes shallow when a certain name appears on your phone. The flatness that settles in after you hang up the phone or when you walk into that building. The strange lightness you feel after you finally say no. You've been minimizing those signals, explaining them away, calling yourself "too sensitive."

This season asks you to treat them as data—because they're telling you the difference between a relationship that can be healed with honest work and one that needs a clean ending to stop the bleeding.

The 'time to kill' in this season has nothing to do with revenge. You're not swinging a sword — you're finally stopping the bleeding.

The Quiet Violence of Leaving What's Wrong

Ending something that has been normal for a long time rarely feels clean or heroic. It feels like confusion, guilt, and grief. You will hear old voices: "You're overreacting." "You're too sensitive." "You're giving up." "You're the problem." You may look at people who stay and wonder why they can tolerate what you cannot.

What feels like a personal flaw is often your system finally refusing to carry what it was never meant to hold.

The "time to kill" can look like blocking a number you used to answer at any hour. Closing a browser tab that leads you somewhere that corrodes your soul. Handing in a resignation letter to a job that pays well but erodes you daily. Telling a parent, sibling, partner, or friend: *"If this continues, I will not stay in this relationship the same way."*

There may be no raised voices, no dramatic scenes, nothing that looks like TV conflict. But emotionally and spiritually, this ending is radical. It is you choosing life over slow erosion.

Ancient healers understood the same principle in a different language: infected flesh had to be lanced so fresh blood could reach what was dying. Sacred texts carried the same pattern—the idols must be torn down before the temple can be restored; the diseased branch cut back before the tree bears good fruit. Across centuries, the message has been consistent: you cannot heal what you refuse to expose, and you cannot save what is poisoning the body. The cut is not the failure of love. It is often where real love finally begins.

Your body already knows this. It has been staging its own quiet protest for longer than you've been willing to admit.

Killing vs. Murder

We need to make a clear distinction.

Killing, in emotional terms, is the conscious removal of something causing ongoing harm—even if it once helped you, even if you have history with it, even if others don't understand. It ends what cannot be made safe and prevents real healing.

Murder is destroying something that still has life in it. It looks like giving up on relationships that need honest communication, abandoning dreams that need patience, and ending things from fear or fatigue rather than wisdom.

The difference is timing and intention. One ends what is already gone. The other abandons what still had a chance. Ending a friendship because it has become genuinely toxic is killing. Ending it because they challenged you on something true is murder. Killing happens when something is already dying, and prolonging it causes more damage. Murder happens when you're too impatient or too scared to do the healing work that's required.

This season is about learning that difference—in your relationships, your habits, and your inner life.

When Love Looks Like Letting Go

Robert came to me after his third anxiety attack at a family gathering. His mother had been emotionally abusive his entire life—constant criticism disguised as concern, guilt weaponized as control, complete dismissal of any boundary he tried to set.

"But she's my mother," he said. *"Family is family. Maybe if I explain better, try harder..."*

He had tried everything, therapy, family counseling, carefully written letters, and temporary distance. Nothing changed. His mother still called him selfish for having needs, still recruited relatives into the narrative that he was "troubled," and still triggered panic attacks with a single text. That relationship wasn't wounded. It was poisonous. It didn't need healing—it needed surgical removal.

Over six months, Robert performed relationship surgery—not with one explosive confrontation, but with a quiet series of non-participations. He stopped answering calls. Stopped attending gatherings. Stopped explaining himself.

His family called him cruel. His mother played the victim. Relatives predicted he'd regret it.

But Robert's panic attacks stopped. There were months when he wondered if he'd made a terrible mistake. That doubt wasn't evidence he had. His health improved. He started dating again, got promoted at work, and his other relationships deepened because he was no longer being drained by one toxic connection. His relationship with his mother had to die completely for Robert to live. Sometimes the most loving thing you can do—for everyone involved—is to stop participating in sickness.

The Art of Emotional Triage

Emergency rooms treat people by urgency, not by who arrived first. Your emotional life needs the same kind of triage.

Emergency surgery: Relationships or patterns that are actively damaging your mental health, self-worth, or safety. These require decisive action—your "time to kill."

Ongoing treatment: Wounded but fundamentally healthy relationships that need work, support, and repair—not demolition.

Natural healing: Minor conflicts and misunderstandings that will resolve with time, honesty, and basic care.

The Yoruba tradition speaks of knowing the difference between 'ogun' — medicine — and 'majele' — poison. The same substance can be either, depending on the dose and the timing. Your discernment is the difference.

Most of us get this backwards. We perform emergency surgery on situations that just need patience, and we slap band-aids on situations that are killing us. This season teaches you to tell the difference.

Your Survival Strategies Are Showing

Relationships aren't the only things that outlive their usefulness. Some of your most loyal survival strategies have become your quietest enemies.

Some behaviors were brilliant survival strategies for an earlier season. They kept you safe in chaotic homes, unsafe workplaces, and inconsistent relationships. But what kept you alive then may be slowly shrinking your life now.

The reflexive *yes* that once kept you from being abandoned is now killing your ability to prioritize what matters. The perfectionism that once protected you from criticism is now suffocating your creativity and risk-taking. The numbing—overwork, scrolling, substances, compulsions—that once helped you cope is now blocking you from joy, intimacy, and presence. Underneath these habits live the thoughts that trained them: "If I say no, they'll leave." "If I'm not perfect, I'm unlovable." "I can't handle this feeling." Those aren't background noise. They are operating systems.

Letting these thoughts die means noticing them when they show up, naming them as expired stories, and refusing to obey them. Their death is not one dramatic moment—it is a long series of quiet refusals. And killing the habit alone is never enough. You also have to plant healthy patterns in the space they leave: boundaries where automatic yeses lived, self-compassion where self-contempt shouted, grounding practices where numbing used to take over.

When Healing Looks Like Destruction

Sometimes healing looks so destructive from the outside that people think you're falling apart when you're finally coming together. When you start setting boundaries with family, they may call you cold. When you quit a prestigious job that is crushing your spirit, they may call you irresponsible. When you end the relationship everyone thought was perfect, they may think you've lost your mind.

What they don't see is that real healing isn't just about feeling better, it's about changing the conditions so the original wound can't keep happening. You cannot heal from codependency while maintaining codependent dynamics. You cannot recover from burnout while keeping the same commitments. You cannot develop self-worth while staying in environments that constantly devalue you. And if you're watching someone you love do this right now, and it looks like chaos — consider that you might be witnessing a surgery you don't have the full chart for.

Healing often requires dismantling the very systems that made you sick. The people watching from outside may never understand that. You don't need them to.

What Gets Released Gets Redirected

Every act of conscious destruction frees energy for conscious creation. The energy once spent managing a toxic relationship can now nourish healthy ones. The mental space consumed by a job you despised can now support meaningful work. The emotional bandwidth drained by numbing can now fuel growth and genuine connection.

But that redirection is not automatic. If you end something harmful without choosing what to grow in its place, leave the space empty long enough, and your old life will walk right back in and sit down like it never left, which is usually the very thing you just escaped. The Zulu concept of 'Ubuntu' — 'I am because we are' — reminds us that what we release doesn't just free us. It frees everyone connected to us. The energy you stop pouring into what is broken becomes available to everyone who needs the healthiest version of you.

Killing and healing must work together. This season does not ask you to be only a destroyer or only a healer. It asks you to become both, in the right order, at the right time.

Reading the Signs

This distinction will change everything.

Signs something needs to be killed:

- You've tried multiple genuine approaches over time and nothing changes meaningfully.
- It consistently damages your mental or physical health.
- It requires you to betray your core values to maintain it.
- It prevents other parts of your life from thriving.
- The cost of keeping it far exceeds any real benefit.

Signs something needs healing, not killing:

- There is mutual willingness to do hard work.
- You see genuine, if slow, progress.
- The foundation is sound even if the surface is cracked.
- Both sides can acknowledge harm and take responsibility.
- It still holds real value, not just history.

Your mind will negotiate. It always does. But negotiation and wisdom are not the same thing. "What if I'm wrong? What if nothing replaces this? What if they change the moment I leave?" Your body and your deeper self already know where the tumors are and where the bruises are. Tumors need removal. Bruises need time, care, and protection. Learning to tell the difference is one of the most important skills you will ever develop.

What you're building in this season is **emotional courage** — the willingness to act on what you already know, even when that knowledge is inconvenient, costly, or deeply unpopular with people you love. Emotional courage is not the absence of fear. It is the decision to move anyway, because staying costs you more than leaving, and protecting what is harming you is no longer something you can call love. Most people know what needs to end long before they end it. They know which habit is destroying them, which relationship has become unsafe, which role they've outgrown. What they lack is not clarity — it's the courage to treat that clarity as valid. This season is where you stop waiting for permission from the outside world to do what your interior world has been requesting for years.

This season gives you permission to stop maintaining what is quietly killing you — the relationship, the role, the habit, the story. You don't need a court ruling. You don't need everyone's blessing. You need the courage to trust what you already know.

If you only remember one thing from this season: What it asks in return is equally simple: don't waste the clearing. Build something in the space. Protect your healing the way you'd protect anything new and worth having — carefully, deliberately, without apology. The Healer and the Surgeon have always lived inside you. This season is just the first time you've been asked to let them work together.

Season Practice: The Surgery Assessment

Name Your Season

Take five minutes. Make two lists—three things that may need killing (clear endings) and three that may need healing (restoration and repair).

Needs to be Killed (ended):

1.

2.

3.

Needs to be Healed (restored):

1.

2.

3.

Notice Your Mind

Write down exactly what your mind says in protest.

- About killing: "If I end this..."

- About healing: "If I stay and work on this..."

Seeing these sentences on the page helps you recognize fear and guilt for what they are, not truth.

Notice Your Body

Think about ending what needs to die. Where do you feel relief—even if it's mixed with fear? Chest, shoulders, jaw, stomach? Now think about committing to healing something that's wounded but still precious. Where do you feel a grounded yes, even if it's hard? Your body knows the difference between relief and resignation.

One Aligned Action This Week

Choose one small action in each category:

If killing: stop one maintenance behavior—a reply, a visit, a scroll, a drink—that keeps a harmful pattern alive.

If healing: add one supportive behavior—a call to a therapist, a walk, a journal entry, a vulnerable conversation—that moves you toward restoration.

Wound and Remedy:
Questions for the Healer Within

Where have you been confusing endurance with healing? What would it mean to stop tolerating something and actually end it?

What is one wound in your life that genuinely deserves to be healed—not ended, but tended? What would that tending look like this week?

Season Summary

> Killing what harms you is the first step of real healing—not a failure of love.
> Some things must die so you can live. Some things must be healed so they don't die unnecessarily.
> Your mind will confuse loyalty with self-abandonment. Your body and intuition know the difference.
> The surgeon's cut and the healer's touch are both acts of love when used with wisdom.
> You are not called to be only a destroyer or only a healer—this season asks you to become both.

Season Four:
A Time to Break Down & A Time to Build Up

There are seasons when the problem isn't how hard you're trying, it's what you're trying to hold up. You keep adding new habits, better routines, more discipline, but the same exhaustion and quiet dread follow you from job to job, relationship to relationship, city to city. It's like living in a house that looks fine from the street but creaks at night, leaks when it rains, and never quite lets you rest. You can rearrange the furniture all you want. Some people have been redecorating for decades. At some point, the structure itself must be addressed.

This is the season of breaking down and building up. Not "breaking down" as in collapsing emotionally—but as in conscious demolition: choosing to dismantle what cannot hold you. Not "building up" as in adding more to your plate—but as in constructing a life that fits your actual self instead of the version other people designed.

The Difference Between Collapse and Choice

To move wisely in this season, you need to understand the difference between falling apart and breaking down on purpose.

Falling apart is what happens when you ignore the cracks until the whole structure gives way. Life overwhelms you, control slips, and you find yourself in emotional rubble without ever choosing to be there. One day you're "fine," and the next you can't stop crying, can't concentrate, can't pretend anymore.

Conscious breakdown is different. It starts with a structural assessment. You step back from your life and ask hard questions: Is this stable, or just familiar? Is this safe, or just survivable? Does this setup honor my values, or mainly other people's expectations?

When you realize the frame itself is wrong, the beams are bowed, the foundation is cracked, the load is more than the design can bear—you stop calling it "fine" and start telling yourself the truth.

Breakdown, in this sense, is proactive. It's the decision to dismantle what cannot be made sound, instead of waiting for it to collapse on you. From the outside, both falling apart and conscious breakdown can look messy. From the inside, one is devastation you didn't choose. The other is courage you finally did.

Living in an Inherited House

Every life is built on blueprints—and most of us never consciously choose ours.

We inherit plans from family, culture, religion, and early experiences long before we have the language to question them. Your family's blueprint might say: get a stable job, marry by a certain age, buy a house, don't rock the boat. Your culture adds: always be productive, never show weakness, measure success in money and status, stay busy so you don't feel too much. Your community or church layers on serve constantly, never disappoint, and sacrifice yourself for others.

So, you build. Degree, job, relationship, mortgage, responsibilities. On paper, it looks like progress. But inside, something feels off. You have shelter, but it doesn't feel like home. You have a role, but not a sense of self. You wake up with the sinking feeling that you're living someone else's life very competently.

The Confucian tradition calls this 'li' — the inherited ritual structure of life that tells you how to behave before you've decided who to be. Following without examination, it builds a perfectly correct life that belongs to someone else.

That chronic misalignment between inherited blueprints and your actual design is what you've probably labeled "burnout," "boredom," or "I guess this is just adulthood." Season Four calls it what it is: a structural problem, not a personal defect. When you finally admit, "This house was built for a version of me that no longer exists," demolition stops feeling reckless and starts feeling merciful.

The House With No Air In It

Amara's life looked enviable. She was a partner at a respected firm, owned a home in a good neighborhood, and had photos from vacations that looked like advertisements. Her parents were proud. Her résumé read like a success story.

Inside, she was suffocating. The gap between how her life looked and how it felt had become so wide she'd stopped trying to explain it, even to herself. She woke with anxiety most mornings. She cycled through stress-related health issues no doctor could fully explain. *I keep thinking—if this is winning, why do I feel like I'm losing myself?"*

As we talked, we began to examine her blueprints. Whose idea of success was she living? What did *she* actually want her days to feel like—not her highlight reel, her Tuesday afternoons?

She lit up when she talked about mentoring younger attorneys, teaching, and working on pro-bono cases. She dimmed when she talked about billable hours, internal politics, and being on call around the clock. The life she'd built fit her parents' dreams perfectly. It did not fit the woman she had become.

"I can't just throw all this away," she said. *"What kind of person does that?"*

We sat with that for a while. Eventually she whispered: *"Maybe I'm not throwing my life away. Maybe I'm just finally admitting this version is a beautiful house I can't breathe in.*

That sentence was the sound of her season beginning. Not when she resigned, not when she sold anything—but when she stopped gaslighting herself about how it felt to live in the structure she'd built.

Conscious breakdown always starts with telling the truth.

The Season of Demolition

Demolition in this season is usually quieter than the movies make it look. There's rarely a single dramatic moment where you shout, "I'm done!" and walk away while music plays. More often, it's a series of small, resolute decisions.

You begin to withdraw from roles that only work if you disappear inside them. You say no to obligations built entirely on guilt and fear. You end patterns of over-functioning that require you to be the emotional scaffolding for everyone else. You step away from environments that look impressive but constantly ask you to trade your health, integrity, or soul for the right to stay.

From the outside, people may say, *"Why would you walk away from that?"* They see the curb appeal. They don't go to sleep in your body at night.

Demolition isn't a wrecking ball swung in anger. It's the quiet, deliberate removal of what was never going to hold you. For one person, that might be a job title. For another, a public persona as "the strong one." For another, a marriage held together by pretending, or a role you stayed in only because no one else would fill it.

What looks like a midlife crisis from the outside is often just a soul that finally stopped lying about its load-bearing capacity.

Standing in the Rubble

After demolition, there is always a phase that feels like failure: the rubble stage.

The old walls are gone. The new ones aren't framed yet. The routines that made you feel competent have ended; new rhythms haven't formed. You may not have a neat answer when someone asks, *"So what do you do?"* You might feel exposed, untethered, and embarrassed.

This is where many people panic and rush to rebuild the old house as fast as possible. The discomfort of open space feels worse than the familiarity of cramped rooms. In terms of building terms, this is just mid-project. Debris has to be cleared before a new foundation can be poured.

In your life, the rubble stage looks like letting go of stories that once kept you safe but now keep you small. It looks like grieving what you invested in a structure that no longer works. It looks like feeling the vulnerability of not having a ready-made identity to hide inside.

You may think, *"I've ruined everything."* You haven't. The Japanese aesthetic of 'ma' — the art of negative space — teaches that emptiness between structures is not absence. It is potentially made visible. You've simply reached the honest middle. The old house is gone; the new one isn't visible yet. That space is not evidence of failure—it is evidence that you stopped pretending.

Excavation

Once the visible structure is down, you can finally see what was buried underneath: the beliefs that held the old house together.

You start to hear the sentences running beneath your choices:

- **"My worth is in my productivity."**
- **"If I disappoint people, I'll be abandoned."**
- **"If I rest, I'm falling behind."**
- **"Conflict means I've failed."**
- **"If I'm not needed, I'll be forgotten."**

Most of these were handed to you before you were old enough to refuse them.

These beliefs were the rebar in your old foundation. As long as they stay unchallenged, any new life you build will quietly recreate the old one with nicer finishes. The zip code changes. Overworking moves with you. The relationship ends. The self-erasure finds the next one. Until you pull up the belief underneath, the house just gets rebuilt in a different neighborhood.

Excavation is uncomfortable because it requires admitting: "The problem isn't only out there—it's also in here." Not as shame, but as clarity. You begin to see how you were taught to overbuild for others and underbuild for yourself.

Naming these beliefs out loud is like pulling up old pipes you didn't know were rusted. It's messy. It's also the only way to make sure the next house doesn't run on the same contaminated system.

What Real Construction Actually Requires

The materials for a conventional life and the materials for an honest one are not the same list. Instead of external markers of success, you need internal resources like self-awareness, courage, resilience, and trust in your own judgment.

Every culture that has ever built anything lasting knew this: the visible structure is only as good as the invisible materials that made it possible.

Self-awareness is your surveying equipment—it helps you assess the landscape of your authentic needs and desires so you know what you're trying to build and where it should be located.

Courage is your heavy machinery—it provides the power to tear down structures that aren't serving you and the strength to build something new even when you don't know exactly how it will turn out.

Resilience is your safety equipment—it protects you when construction gets difficult, when people question your choices, or when building takes longer than expected.

Trust in your own judgment is your master blueprint. It guides every decision about what to keep, what to remove, and what to build from scratch.

Patience is your timeline management. It helps you understand that authentic building takes time and that trying to rush the process usually creates structural problems that must be fixed later.

Community support is your foundation. It provides a stable base that allows you to take risks and make changes without losing your footing entirely.

Building these internal resources is part of the construction process. These materials grow through use. You do not wait until you "have enough courage" to start; courage develops as you make courageous choices.

Building with Intention

After demolition and excavation comes the part most people don't expect to be this hard: building something new with no inherited blueprint to follow.

You're not here to rebuild the same house with better finishes. You're here to design something that fits the person you've become. That starts with discovering your authentic blueprints. What energizes versus drains you? If you've spent years building for others, these questions can feel genuinely foreign at first. That disorientation is not a sign something is wrong — it's a sign you're asking them for the first time. What relationships feel real versus performed? When does work feel like a genuine contribution versus an obligation?

Your authentic blueprints probably look nothing like anyone else's. Maybe you need more solitude than society says is healthy. Less structure than success supposedly requires. Work rhythms that don't match corporate schedules. Success metrics that have nothing to do with money. Building authentically means constructing life structures that support those needs instead of fighting them.

This phase is slower than you want it to be. Instead of asking "What will impress people?" you ask "What can my soul sustainably hold?" Instead of "What looks successful?" you ask, "What feels like home?" You begin testing new beams: work that aligns with your values, relationships where you can tell the truth and still be loved, rhythms that include real rest rather than just collapse. At first, your new structures may look smaller from the outside—less income, fewer commitments, a simpler calendar. To people still building by the old blueprints, it may look like you've downsized. Inside, it feels like space to breathe for the first time.

What you're building in this season is emotional flexibility — the capacity to tolerate the uncomfortable in-between space where the old structure is down and the new one is not yet standing. Most people underestimate how disorienting this feels. They expect demolition to feel like relief and construction to feel like progress. What they don't anticipate is the exposure: the openness, the uncertainty, the nakedness of a life mid-renovation.

Emotional flexibility is what keeps you from rushing back to old blueprints just because the open space feels unbearable. It is the ability to say "I don't know what this will look like yet" without that uncertainty collapsing into panic. The people who build lives they actually love are not the ones who had the clearest plan — they are the ones who could stay in the mess long enough for something honest to emerge.

Your Emotional Construction Crew

Nobody builds alone. And not everyone qualifies for your crew. Many people will try to hand you back the old blueprints. *"This is how it's done,"* they'll say. *"This is what works."* They mean well, but they're offering conventional materials for an unconventional build.

Your crew needs people who have built unconventionally and survived. Friends who celebrate your authentic self, not your performance. Mentors who ask, *"What do you want?"* rather than *"What should you want?"* Professionals who support transformation, not just adjustment.

Some people will try to talk you back into the old house because your renovation unsettles their comfort. Others will project their own fears onto your courage. The Māori concept of 'whakapapa' — knowing where you come from, so you know where you're going — reminds us that the people who belong in your story are the ones who honor your becoming, not just your belonging. Your real crew are the ones who ask, *"How can I support this?"* rather than *"Why would you risk that?"*

Be selective about who sees the construction site. Not every person in your life is a construction-site relationship. Some are meant for the finished rooms.

One Room at a Time

You don't have to demolish and rebuild everything at once. Complete life renovation is a television fantasy. Real change happens incrementally.

Start with one room. Maybe your evenings—stop filling them with obligations and start protecting them for what you want. The West African proverb says: 'Rain does not fall on one roof alone.' Change that begins in one corner of your life has a way of eventually reaching everything else. One authentic change creates momentum for the next.

Each structure that genuinely supports who you are makes it easier to recognize what doesn't fit. Each small, aligned build—a boundary, a habit, a relationship, a new routine—reinforces your new blueprint and quietly weakens your attachment to the old one.

The foundation this season creates is not perfection. It's confidence. Confidence that if structures crack again, you know how to assess, dismantle, and rebuild. Confidence that you are not trapped by old blueprints. Your inner architect has been sketching your real life for years. Your inner contractor is ready to start. The only question is whether you'll trust yourself enough to pick up the tools.

If you only remember one thing from this season: The life that looks fine from the street but makes you dread waking up is not a personal failure, it's a structural problem. You are allowed to stop pretending the cracks aren't there. You are allowed to break it down and build something that fits. The only person who can authorize that renovation is you.

Season Practice: The Blueprint Assessment

You don't have to bulldoze your entire life to honor this season. You do need to start seeing like an architect instead of just a resident. Choose one area of your life to assess right now—a job, a key role in your family, a relationship, a community commitment, or even an identity you live from like "the strong one" or "the fixer."

Name Your Season

Write one sentence:

"The house I'm assessing is my role as ____________."

Notice Your Mind

Answer these structural questions honestly on paper:

- Does this feel stable, or just familiar?
- Does this feel safe, or just survivable?
- Does this align with my deepest values, or mostly with other people's expectations?

Notice which answers make your body tighten. That's where the beams are bowed.

Notice Your Body

Think about continuing to maintain this structure exactly as it is. Notice where your body goes first — not what your mind says, what your body does. That response is structural information.

One Aligned Action This Week

Choose one small action from each of these:

One brick of demolition: Stop one way you're reinforcing a structure that doesn't fit. Don't volunteer automatically. Pause before you say yes. Admit to one trusted person, *"This isn't working for me the way it looks like it is."*

One new beam: What would a slightly more honest version of this area of your life look like—just for now? Name one concrete change: a boundary, a schedule adjustment, a clarified expectation, one step toward a different path.

Demolition and Design:
What Are You Ready to Rebuild?

Whose blueprint have you been building from? What would you design differently if you started from who you actually are today?

What's the belief buried underneath the structure you're maintaining? Say it out loud, write it down. Is it true—or is it just old?

Season Summary

- Falling apart is a collapse you didn't choose. Conscious breakdown is demolition you choose when a structure can't be made sound.
- You've been building on inherited blueprints—family, culture, community—that may no longer fit who you are.
- The fact that your life works on paper doesn't mean it works for your soul. Chronic friction is a structural signal, not a personal failure.
- Demolition is rarely dramatic—it's often a series of quiet decisions to stop supporting roles and environments that require your self-erasure.
- The rubble stage—when the old is gone and the new isn't visible yet—is not proof you ruined everything. It's what every construction site looks like mid-project.
- Hidden beliefs like *"My worth is my productivity"* were the rebar holding your old life in place. If you don't excavate them, any new life you build will quietly recreate the old one.
- Building up means designing a life that matches your values, limits, and actual desires, not what looks impressive from the outside.
- The question is no longer "How do I keep this going?" It's "What kind of house can actually hold the weight of who I am becoming?"

MOVEMENT THREE: EMOTIONAL FLUENCY

Mastering Your Internal Weather

The first two Movements asked hard things of you. They asked you to face endings, clear what was overgrown, and stop participating in what was harming you. Now the work changes direction. You've let some things die so others can be born. You've uprooted what was choking your growth, ended what was harming you, and begun building structures that actually fit who you are becoming. Now the work moves inward.

The ancient Egyptians believed the heart — the 'ib' — was the seat of intelligence, conscience, and will. Not the head. The heart. They weighed it at the end of a life not because it was unreliable but because it was the most honest thing a person carried.

This Movement is about learning to live inside your own heart without treating it as an enemy, a problem to fix, or a performance to manage. The question shifts from 'How do I stop feeling this?' to 'What is this feeling trying to tell me, and what does it need from me right now? Emotional fluency is a more honest and skillful relationship with the emotions you already have. Not fewer feelings. Better conversations with them.

The Cost of Editing Your Feelings

Most of us weren't raised to be fluent in our inner world; we were raised to be presentable. Somewhere along the way, you picked up rules: sadness makes you weak or ungrateful, so fix it or hide it. Joy during hard times is inappropriate, like you're being disrespectful to the pain. Anger is dangerous unless it's distant and abstract. Mixed emotions mean you're confused, dramatic, or just too much.

Under those rules, your life becomes an editing project. You apologize when your eyes fill with tears. You downplay excitement so you don't make anyone uncomfortable. You swallow discomfort because you don't want to ruin the moment. From the outside, it can look like composure. On the inside, it feels like slowly disappearing inside your own life.

Emotional fluency offers a different path. Sadness becomes a report about what matters, not a defect. Joy is fuel, not a luxury you have to earn. Anger is sometimes an alarm telling you a boundary has been crossed. Mixed emotions are reality, not a malfunction. The goal isn't to make your heart simpler; it is to become more skilled at listening to it.

The Seasons of Your Inner Weather

Movement Three turns to the weather inside you. Ecclesiastes names several pairings that sound like events, but they describe inner climates just as much as outer ones:

A time to weep and a time to laugh is about tears and laughter as tools, not just reactions. Most people are waiting for permission to do either one fully. This Movement is that permission. Weeping lets grief move instead of calcifying. Laughter lets joy and relief breathe instead of shrinking under the weight of seriousness. Emotional fluency means you stop apologizing for either one—and stop insisting only one is allowed at a time.

A time to mourn and a time to dance is about emotions too big to carry alone. Emotions that have been witnessed settle differently than emotions that have only been processed alone. Mourning is grief made communal. Dancing is joy shared and amplified. Both say, "This matters enough that I can't hold it by myself." Emotional fluency means knowing when you need someone to sit with you in sorrow, or someone to celebrate with you in joy—so your feelings have room to breathe.

A time to cast away stones and a time to gather them is about what you carry emotionally. Casting away looks like releasing grudges, false responsibilities, and outdated stories about who you are. Gathering looks like intentionally collecting experiences, truths, and relationships that can serve as foundations. Emotional fluency means becoming a curator of your inner landscape—choosing what stays and what goes.

A time to tear and a time to mend is about the emotional fabric of your life. Tearing is the honest acknowledgment: "This hurt me." "This isn't working." "This broke something in me." Mending is the work of stitching trust back together, weaving new meaning, integrating what happened so it becomes part of your story rather than the whole of it.

Emotional fluency means you don't rush to mend when something still needs to be named—and you don't keep tearing the same fabric long after it's ready to be repaired.

What Emotional Fluency Is Not

Before we step into these seasons one by one, let's be clear about what this Movement is *not* asking of you. It is not an invitation to become more dramatic, share everything with everyone, or let your feelings drive every decision. High drama is not fluency—it's often a way of acting out pain without understanding it.

Emotional fluency is also not a new form of perfectionism. You will still get flooded, still shut down sometimes, still say "I'm fine" when you're not. Those moments aren't failure—they're the raw material we're working with. The goal was never to become someone who processes feelings perfectly. The goal is to become someone who stops being afraid of them.

And this Movement is not about ignoring your history. The Lakota understanding of 'wacante ogankiye' — generosity of heart toward oneself — holds that the same compassion you would offer a child learning something difficult for the first time is exactly what this work requires of you. If you grew up in a home where emotions were mocked, weaponized, or met with silence, learning a new way will take time and tenderness. You are not behind. You are doing work that many before you didn't have the language or the safety to do.

Your emotional life is one of your most accurate sources of information, connection, and guidance. This Movement is where you finally start treating it that way.

The central shift is simple to write and hard to live: you stop asking "How do I get rid of this feeling?" and start asking "What season is this feeling in, and what does that season need?"

You will not become someone who never feels overwhelmed or conflicted. You will become someone who, when the waves rise inside, knows how to say: "I recognize this water. I know how to swim here."

Season Five:
A Time to Weep & Time to Laugh

There are seasons when the most important work is not changing your job, your relationship, or your location—it's changing your permission to feel. Everything outside you might look functional, even successful, yet inside you feel pressured. Like a bottle that's been shaken for years with the cap screwed on tight. At some point, the pressure itself becomes the new normal — and you stop noticing how much energy it takes just to keep the cap on. Tears come at inconvenient times and get swallowed. Laughter bursts out and is immediately toned down. You keep trying to manage your emotions instead of listening to them.

This is the season where you learn that weeping and laughing are not evidence that you're unstable. They are how your soul moves energy, honors what matters, and stays human in a world that keeps telling you to stay composed.

The Rules You Learned About Feelings

Very few of us grew up hearing, *"Your emotions are welcome exactly as they are."* Instead, we absorbed rules—spoken or implied—about what was acceptable to feel and when.

Maybe you learned that sadness should be hidden. You heard, "Stop crying or I'll give you something to cry about," or "Go to your room and come back when you've calmed down." You discovered that tears made adults uncomfortable or angry, so you taught yourself to shut them off or allow them only in private.

Maybe joy had rules too. "Don't brag." "Don't get your hopes up." "Don't be too happy, it never lasts." You learned to downplay your excitement, to be suspicious of good things, to feel almost disloyal if you smiled while someone you loved was still struggling.

Some families made anger the only safe emotion, tears were mocked, tenderness felt dangerous, but rage was allowed. And some families had no room for any of it, where the most dangerous thing you could do was need something out loud.

Other families did the opposite: anger was forbidden, so frustration leaked out as anxiety, people-pleasing, or relentless self-criticism.

By adulthood, you've internalized an emotional etiquette: don't cry here, don't laugh there, don't feel too much of anything for too long. The cost is that your nervous system never gets to complete its natural cycles. Grief gets stuck instead of moving through. Joy flares up and dies before it can nourish you.

Season Five arrives to rewrite those rules.

The Myth of One Emotion at a Time

From an early age, most of us are trained into an emotional myth: mature adults are supposed to be clear, contained, and consistent. If you're sad, be sad. If you're happy, be happy. Don't send mixed signals. Don't ruin a moment with the wrong feeling.

So, you start to self-police. You swallow tears because you don't want to be dramatic. You dim your joy because you don't want to be inappropriate. You become a careful curator of your own heart, sorting feelings into acceptable and unacceptable piles before anyone else can judge you.

Or maybe you're on the other side—so disconnected from your feelings that you can't cry when you need to or laugh when something's genuinely funny. You've become so good at keeping it together that you've forgotten how to fall apart.

But real life never signed that contract. Reality does not present itself in single-emotion scenes. You can feel genuine relief and deep devastation in the same hour. You can miss someone so fiercely it steals your breath and still feel quietly grateful they're no longer suffering. You can celebrate a promotion while grieving the version of yourself who stayed small for years just to be liked.

Either way, you end up in the same gray corridor — functional on the outside, quietly starving on the inside: emotional constipation that turns into anxiety, numbness, or the low-grade depression that colors everything gray.

The tears you don't cry become weird feelings in your chest. The joy you don't express becomes bitterness that keeps you from receiving good things.

Emotional honesty means admitting that your heart rarely lives in just one feeling at a time. It's closer to a whole orchestra tuning up than a single instrument playing alone. It's time to trust that complexity instead of shaming it.

The ancient Greeks had two words for time: 'chronos,' clock time, and 'kairos,' the right moment. Emotional life runs almost entirely on kairos. It arrives when it arrives, not when your schedule permits.

When Your Body Tells the Truth First

Tears and laughter are your body's way of saying: *"Something significant just moved inside me."* Your mind might be trying to stay on schedule, stay appropriate, stay in control—but your nervous system is not interested in performance. It is interested in truth.

The Aboriginal Australians speak of 'dadirri' — a deep inner listening, a quiet waiting that allows truth to surface from within rather than being forced from without. Your tears and laughter are surfacing.

Think about the last time you cried "out of nowhere." Maybe it was a song, a commercial, a throwaway scene in a show where someone finally said the thing you've been longing to hear. On paper, nothing new had happened. Your mind insisted you were fine. Your eyes disagreed.

Or think about the last time you laughed harder than you meant to. The joke wasn't that brilliant. You weren't in an easy season. But something about the timing, the look on someone's face, the shared absurdity in the room, it cracked something open. You laughed until your stomach hurt, and for a moment, the heaviness you'd been carrying loosened its grip.

In both cases, your body was telling you: "There is more going on here than your conscious mind has words for." Weeping often shows up when the pain you postponed finally finds a door. Laughter often shows up when joy, relief, or absurdity needs an outlet before you collapse under the weight of too much seriousness.

Emotional fluency in this season begins with treating those signals as the most honest thing happening in the room.

The Different Dialects of Sorrow

Tears don't all speak the same language. Learning to hear the difference changes how you respond to yourself when they arrive.

Grief tears are deep, body-shaking sobs for loss. They reorganize your life around absence.

Release tears come when you've held something too heavy for too long—often after stress ends, your body finally exhales, "I can stop bracing now."

Overwhelm tears aren't really about sadness, they're your nervous system creating a pause to discharge and reset when you've hit your capacity.

Compassion tears are when beauty or love moves you. These are tears of connection to something larger than yourself.

Healing tears come when something frozen finally thaws—when what was too dangerous to feel before becomes safe enough to release.

The Dagara people of West Africa build entire community rituals around grief, understanding that unexpressed sorrow doesn't disappear — it migrates into the body and the collective until it is witnessed.

Each type serves a different function. You're not falling apart. You're completing a process.

The Liberation of Laughter

Laughter is just as sophisticated as tears, and just as necessary. Performative happiness is a management strategy. Authentic joy is an arrival. You can tell the difference because one exhausts you and the other feeds you. Performative happiness is a strategy, a people-pleasing tool, a way of managing other people's discomfort with your reality. Authentic joy is presence. It's being open to moments of delight even in imperfect circumstances.

When you laugh genuinely—not polite social laughter, but deep, surprising, belly-shaking laughter—your body floods with oxygen, releases endorphins, and your muscles relax in waves. Your perspective shifts. Laughter doesn't minimize your problems. It reminds you that even in difficulty, absurdity, and lightness still exist, if you're willing to notice them.

The Pattern That Keeps You Numb

When you fight the season of weeping and laughing, you fall into one of two exhausting patterns.

In the first, you clamp down. You keep your face neutral, your tone even, your calendar full. You tell yourself you're staying strong, and you might even feel proud of how rarely things "get to you." Inside, though, unexpressed grief hardens into cynicism and fatigue.

Uncelebrated joys evaporate before they can nourish you. People may describe you as reliable and competent, but few would say they feel truly close to you.

In the second pattern, you swing. Because you have no steady practice of feeling in real time, emotions build pressure until they erupt. You don't cry for months, then sob uncontrollably and feel ashamed of it. You keep it together in public, then explode at home over something minor. Or you chase high after high—because steady calm feels too much like numbness to trust.

In both patterns, feelings are treated as problems: either enemies to subdue or episodes that simply happen to you. You rarely experience them as waves that rise, crest, and fall while you stay present through them.

One of the quiet skills you develop in this season is learning to treat your emotions less like verdicts and more like weather reports. You start noticing *"I'm sad"* without immediately deciding something is wrong with you. You start noticing *"I'm laughing"* without assuming it means you must be over it. You begin to realize that weeping and laughing are not commands about who you are, they're signals about what's moving through you.

The Song She Couldn't Skip

Maya liked to joke that she "didn't do crying." Her friends called her a robot when movies made everyone else tear up. She wore it like a badge: *"I just handle things."*

But recently her body had started telling a different story. She had headaches that wouldn't go away. Her sleep was shallow and broken. Small inconveniences made her disproportionately angry. She described herself as stuck but couldn't point to a single event to blame.

In one conversation, she mentioned a song she couldn't listen to anymore. *"I skip it every time,"* she said casually. *"I don't even know why."* It turned out to be a song that played at her father's funeral—a man she'd loved deeply and lost suddenly.

We didn't start by forcing tears. We started with sensation. Where in her body did she feel something when she thought about him? *"My throat,"* she said. *"It tightens."* What happened if she breathed into that place slowly instead of immediately pushing the feeling away? Her eyes started to sting. Her jaw clenched. She laughed it off: *"Wow, I really don't want to go there."*

Over several conversations, she practiced staying with that discomfort for a few seconds at a time—not drowning in it, just not running. One afternoon, she decided to play the song in her car. She had to pull over. She wept so hard she worried she would never stop.
But she did.

Grief, it turns out, is not a bottomless pit. It has a floor.

In the weeks after that drive, her headaches eased. Her anger softened. She found herself actually laughing with friends instead of performing laughter. *"I think I was afraid,"* she said, *"that if I started crying about him, I would fall apart forever. But it turns out I just needed to stop pretending I was fine."*

Her tears didn't erase her loss. They made room for it. They allowed her to live alongside her grief instead of building a wall around it and calling that wall strength.

The Guilt of Laughing When Life Is Hard

If weeping is complicated for some of us, laughing in hard seasons can be just as fraught.

You might know the feeling: you're in the middle of a crisis—uncertain work, a breakup, illness, grief—and something genuinely funny happens. A kid says something unexpected. A friend makes the exact right joke. You laugh, fully, for a moment. Then the guilt kicks in. "How can I laugh right now? Does this mean I didn't love them enough? Am I minimizing my own pain?"

Many of us absorbed the idea that real grief is pure and continuous— that if life is heavy, you should look heavy all the time. Joy in the middle of a struggle feels like betrayal.

But if you've ever sat in genuine grieving spaces—hospital rooms, funerals, living rooms after bad news—you know that's not how human hearts work. In the middle of tears, there is almost always some laughter: a story about the person that is so perfectly them you can't help but smile, an absurd detail that breaks the tension for thirty seconds, a mispronounced word that sends everyone into tired hysterics.

That laughter is oxygen. Your nervous system is taking a breath, so it doesn't go under. It's your nervous system taking a micro-break, so it doesn't shut down. It's love remembering that the person you lost was more than the way they died—and that you are more than what's happening to you right now.

The Irish wake has always known this — that keening and storytelling and laughter around the table are not contradictions. They are the full sound of love refusing to be reduced to a single note.

Emotional fluency in this season means allowing those pockets of light without turning them into a moral verdict on how much you care. You can still be deeply in grief and have real moments of joy. Both can be true, and neither one cancels the other out.

The Shift: Letting Both Live in the Same Room

The central shift of Season Five is accepting that weeping and laughing are not rivals. They are partners keeping you whole.

Instead of asking "Should I be crying or laughing about this?" you begin to say: "Of course I'm crying and laughing in the same week—sometimes about the same thing." Of course, you can feel relief and sadness when a difficult chapter ends. Sufi poets called this 'the ache of aliveness', the bittersweet recognition that to feel anything deeply is to feel everything a little. Of course, you can feel both joy for a friend's good news and a pang for your own unfulfilled longing. Of course, you can grieve what you've lost and still feel grateful for what remains.

You stop putting your own heart on trial. Tears become evidence that you were paying attention. Laughter becomes proof that life can still reach you, even here. You also stop waiting for your feelings to line up into one clean story before you honor them.

You learn to sit with "I don't fully understand what I feel, but something in me needs to move." Sometimes that movement will be crying. Sometimes it will be smiling at something small. Both are forms of truth-telling. Both are forms of staying alive inside your own life.

This is not emotional chaos. It is emotional sophistication. It is a sign that your heart is big enough to hold complexity—instead of flattening yourself to make other people more comfortable.

What you're building in this season is **emotional authenticity** — the ability to let your actual emotional response exist without running it through a filter of what is appropriate, convenient, or socially acceptable. Emotional authenticity does not mean performing your feelings for an audience. It means giving yourself honest internal permission before you decide what to share or how to share it.

It means not immediately overriding the pang you feel with "I shouldn't feel this way," or rushing past the unexpected laugh with "that was inappropriate." Your emotions are not evidence of your character — they are information about your inner landscape. When you stop editing before you feel, you stop losing data about your own life. And the more accurately you can read that data, the more wisely you can move through whatever season you're in.

If you only remember one thing from this season: Tears do not mean you're weak—they mean something mattered. Laughter does not mean you're in denial—it means life can still reach you. You don't have to choose between them. You just have to stop apologizing for whichever one shows up.

Season Practice: Giving Your Heart Permission

Name Your Season

Without judging it, describe today's emotional sky in a simple phrase: "heavy with spots of light," "flat gray," "bright with a storm on the edge," "foggy but warming." You're not trying to be poetic—you're just admitting how it actually feels.

Notice Your Mind

As you do this, listen for the voice that says *"This is stupid," "You're being dramatic,"* or *"You don't have time for this."* Silently name it: *"old training."* You don't have to argue with it—but you also don't have to obey it.

Notice Your Body

Ask yourself: "If my body could express even 5% more of what it feels right now, what might it want to do?" Maybe it wants to sigh deeply, let your shoulders drop, let your eyes water for a few seconds, or let a smile stay on your face without immediately erasing it. Let that happen gently, without commentary.

One Aligned Action This Week

Over the next few days, when a genuine moment of sadness or joy arises with someone you trust, experiment with letting it be visible for one breath longer than usual. Maybe you let your eyes actually fill instead of looking away. Maybe you let your laugh be a little louder instead of clamping down and apologizing. You're not performing— you're practicing.

Weather Report: Questions for Your Emotional Climate

Which emotion has been harder to allow lately—sadness or joy? What rule did you learn that made it harder, and where did that rule come from?

Think of a moment recently when you felt two emotions at once and judged yourself for it. What would it look like to honor both of those feelings instead of choosing one?

Season Summary

- You learned early which emotions were allowed, so you've been editing your sadness and joy to stay acceptable—and it's been costing you.
- Weeping and laughing are your body's way of telling the truth before your mind has the words. They are data, not defects.
- Clamping down leads to numbness and quiet burnout. Swinging between extremes leads to emotional whiplash. There's a third way: feeling in small, honest doses in real time.
- Not all tears are the same. Learning which kind you're having helps you support the process instead of fighting it.
- Grief and joy naturally mix. The guilt about laughing during hard times is learned—not evidence that you don't care.
- Emotional maturity is the capacity to feel more than one thing at once without turning on yourself.
- The question in this season is not "How do I stop feeling this?" but "How can I let this feeling move through me without abandoning myself?"

Season Six:
A Time to Mourn & A Time to Dance

There are seasons when your private tears are no longer enough. You've cried in the car, journaled, prayed, said all the right things in therapy—and yet something in you still feels unfinished. Like grief stuck in mid-sentence. You've done everything the books suggested, and the books weren't wrong; they just weren't the whole answer. You can function. You even have moments of laughter. But the heaviness never fully moves, and joy, when it appears, doesn't seem to stick.

This is the season of mourning and dancing. Not just feeling sad and happy in private but allowing your grief and your joy to become communal experiences instead of solitary ones. In this season, you learn that some emotions are simply too big for one heart to hold alone—they need witnesses, ritual, and shared movement to transform.

Most ancient cultures refused to grieve or celebrate alone. The Egyptians built forty days of communal mourning into their culture — not because grief took exactly forty days, but because they understood that sorrow witnessed by a community transforms differently than sorrow carried alone. Communities hired mourners to cry out loud at funerals, so nobody had to carry sorrow in silence. They held day-long festivals with music and dancing, so joy didn't stay trapped in theory. Their wisdom was simple and inconvenient: some feelings only move through the body when other bodies are present.

Mourning without witnesses becomes despair. Dancing without shared meaning becomes a distraction. So, they built rhythms where grief and celebration were carried together—because they understood something we've largely forgotten: you were never meant to hold the biggest moments of your life entirely by yourself.

The Difference Between Weeping and Mourning

Most of us were never taught the difference between weeping and mourning. We use the words interchangeably and then wonder why our grief doesn't move.

Weeping is weather. It is immediate, bodily, often private. Tears in the grocery store, the sob in the shower, the lump in your throat during a song. Weeping is usually involuntary and focused on release.

Mourning is climate. It is longer, communal, and often ritualized. It looks like funerals, memorials, sitting shiva, anniversaries, gathering to tell stories, lighting candles, visiting a grave together, or creating your own small ceremony. The Hindu tradition of antim sanskar — the final rites — stretches across thirteen days of communal gathering, not to prolong pain but to ensure the living are never alone inside it. Mourning is chosen, witnessed, and focused on meaning-making.

You can weep without mourning—crying alone about a divorce you never let anyone really see. You can mourn without visibly weeping—dry-eyed at a memorial where your presence alone says, *"this mattered."* But transformation usually asks for both: the raw honesty of personal feeling and the stabilizing container of shared acknowledgment.

The same distinction applies to joy. Feeling happy by yourself is beautiful—but dancing, in this season, means any shared, embodied expression of joy: raising your hands in worship, moving to music at a wedding, shouting at a graduation, clinking glasses after a hard-won victory. You can feel joy in private; you dance when you let that joy be seen and amplified by others.

A life of only mourning eventually forgets what it was mourning for. A life of only dancing eventually runs out of things to celebrate. This season asks you to hold the door open for both. This season is about learning to let your heart do both.

When Grief Has No Witnesses

When Sarai's mother died, she did what many emotionally responsible people do. She cried alone in her car, processed her feelings weekly in therapy, journaled late at night, and read every recommended book on grief. Six months later, she wasn't in acute pain anymore—but she also wasn't at peace. She described it as *"a sadness with nowhere to go."*

"I've done everything right," she told me. *"I've felt my feelings. I've honored my grief. Why don't I feel complete?"*

Because she had been weeping. But she had not been mourning.

The following week, eight people who had loved her mother gathered in Sarai's living room. They brought stories, not advice. They laughed about her mother's obsession with QVC jewelry and the way she mispronounced words on purpose just to make people smile. Each person shared one way her mother had shaped their life. At the end, they wrote something they were grateful for on slips of paper and burned them in a small bowl—a letting-go that felt more like gratitude than erasure.

Sarai cried harder that evening than she had in months. But this time, the tears moved somewhere. *"It's like my grief finally had witnesses,"* she said. *"It became real. It became shared. It became bearable."* What Sarai discovered that evening is what every culture that ever built a mourning ritual already knew. That is the shift of this season: your pain and your joy stop living only inside your chest and start living in a room where others can see, hold, and honor them.

The Pattern That Keeps You Alone

When you resist this season, you tend to fall into one of two patterns.

In the first, you try to keep the biggest moments of your life in the smallest possible container: yourself. You grieve deaths alone because everyone has their own grief. You minimize your losses, so you don't burden your friends. You process breakups, miscarriages, and career collapses in private, then show up composed so no one worries. You get promoted, recover from addiction, or survive a terrifying season—and tell almost no one because other people are going through worse. Comparison has become the reason you give yourself permission to feel nothing.

In the second pattern, you perform emotions publicly without letting anyone truly close. You post about your grief on social media but never let anyone sit with you on your couch in silence.

You throw parties for other people's milestones but sidestep any celebration of your own. You attend everyone else's funerals, weddings, and graduations—yet never ask anyone to stand with you for the transitions that are reshaping your life.

Either way the result is the same gray outcome: emotions that never quite integrate, grief that won't lift, joy that won't root. Grief that won't lift. Joy that won't root. The sense that your life keeps turning but your soul is stuck between chapters.

Beneath both patterns run rigid internal rules: "Grief should be private." "If I celebrate, I'm bragging." "You shouldn't laugh at the repast." "You shouldn't cry at the bridal shower." "There's a right amount of time to be sad, and then you should be over it."

The hidden cost is that you're trying to be both the one experiencing the moment and the entire community holding it. That's like trying to be a surgeon and patient at the same time. Some operations require other hands.

The Son Who Forgot to Grieve

Garret's father died suddenly. He flew home, handled the paperwork, coordinated the service, wrote and delivered the eulogy, made sure his mother ate and slept, then went straight back to work. People said, *"You're so strong."*

Months later, he wasn't crying. He wasn't falling apart. He also wasn't sleeping more than a few hours at a time. He woke up most mornings with a dread he couldn't explain. *"I did everything right,"* he said. *"I handled it. Why does it still feel unfinished?"*

As he described the week of the funeral, a pattern emerged. In every story he told, he was the organizer, the problem-solver, the emotional support person—making sure everyone else was okay. In none of them was he simply the son who had lost his dad.

We talked about what mourning—not just weeping—might look like for him. A month later, he invited three close friends over. They ordered his father's favorite takeout and ate it on mismatched plates the way his dad used to insist. They told stories, including the imperfect ones that made them all laugh. They played his father's favorite song and let it play all the way through without talking. At one point, Garret finally let himself cry while someone simply rested a hand on his shoulder. *"It's strange,"* he said afterward. *"I've been talking about him for months. But this is the first time I feel like I actually mourned him."* Nothing about the facts changed. What changed was that his grief moved from a solo loop in his head to a shared experience in a room.

The Navajo tradition speaks of 'hózhó' — a state of balance and beauty restored through ceremony and community. Garret's evening with his friends was hózhó. Informal, imperfect, and exactly right. His role shifted from that of a caretaker to that of a son. That shift belongs to this season.

Dancing After the Valley

If mourning feels risky, dancing again can feel like outright betrayal. Two years after losing her husband, Lila attended her niece's wedding. She told herself she was just going to show her face and leave early. At the reception, the DJ played a song she and her husband used to dance to in their kitchen. Her chest tightened. She stepped toward the exit.

Her niece caught her eye from the dance floor and mouthed, *"Stay."* A moment later, her brother took her hand and gently pulled her into the circle. For the first few seconds, she moved stiffly, tears in her eyes. Then something in her body remembered—the way he used to spin her, the way she used to laugh when she stepped on his toes. Her tears didn't stop. But she kept dancing.

Later that night she said, *"For a second, I felt guilty. Like if anyone saw me smiling, they'd think I didn't miss him anymore. But the weird thing is, I felt closer to him on that dance floor than I have in months. Like he would have been mad if I just sat in the corner and watched life happen without me."*

Dancing in this season—literal or metaphorical—is how you tell the truth that grief hasn't taken everything. You're still here. That deserves its own moment. It is an honor that you are still alive. It is saying: "I carry this loss, and I will also choose moments of joy." It is how you refuse to let grief take everything when it has already taken so much.

Permission to live fully is sometimes the last gift the people we lose are still trying to give us.

The Shift: From Private Pain to Shared Ritual

The central shift of Season Six is moving from "I have to hold this by myself" to "This deserves to be honored with others."

Instead of asking "Why can't I just get over this?" you begin to ask "What would mourning this actually look like—not just feeling it, but marking it?" Instead of thinking "If I celebrate, I'm being insensitive," you ask, "What would it mean to let this joy be seen so it can actually land in my body?"

Private coping strategies are excellent at management. They were never designed for transformation. Your nervous system was built for ritual, the way your lungs were built for air. Self-awareness is useful. Ceremony is nourishment. The ceremony can be ten candles or one. A room full of people or a single friend on your couch. What makes it sacred is the decision to show up for it.

You also release the fantasy of a correct timeline. There is no universal number of months when grief should fade, no point at which missing someone becomes too much, no age at which you lose your right to be celebrated. You can mourn a ten-year-old loss in a new way today. You can dance in the middle of a difficult year because something beautiful still deserves its own moment.

The Jewish concept of 'simcha shel mitzvah' — the joy of doing what is right — holds that celebration in the middle of hardship is not denial. It is an act of spiritual defiance.

What you're building in this season is emotional integration — the process by which scattered, unwitnessed emotional experiences finally become part of a coherent story you can actually carry. Unintegrated emotions don't disappear; they circle. They show up as the persistent sense that you've processed something without ever actually completing it — like a sentence your life started, and your heart never got to finish.

Integration happens when an experience moves from being something that happened inside you, alone, to something that has been seen and held in connection with others.

Grief that has been witnessed settles in a different way than grief that has only been processed. Joy that has been shared roots in a different way than joy that was quietly felt and let pass. This is not a weakness — it is how the human nervous system was designed to function. We are not built to integrate the most significant moments of our lives entirely alone.

Emotional maturity in this season looks like this: you let grief and joy move from private weather inside you to shared climates you walk through with others.

If you only remember one thing from this season: Weeping is something you do alone. Mourning is something you do together. Joy can be felt in private. Dancing is what happens when you let that joy be witnessed. Some of what you've been carrying has been waiting—not for more private processing, but for a room full of people who love you and a reason to finally put it down together.

Season Practice: The Mourning & The Dancing Ritual

You don't need a big event to live this season. You can begin with two simple, intentional acts—one for mourning, one for dancing.

Name Your Season

Make two lists:

One loss that still tugs at me and has never been properly witnessed:

1.

2.

3.

One win, survival, or joy I minimized and never truly celebrated:

1.

2.

3.

Notice Your Mind

Write down what your mind says when you imagine asking someone to witness your grief or celebrate your joy with you.

- About mourning together: "I can't ask someone to do that because..."

- About dancing together: "I can't let myself celebrate that because..."

Those sentences are the rules running the show. Seeing them on paper helps you decide whether to keep following them.

Notice Your Body

Think about one loss you've been carrying alone. Notice where it lives — is it behind your eyes, in the set of your jaw, in the way you're holding your breath right now? Now think about one joy you've kept small. What does your body do when you imagine letting it be seen? Something contracts. Something wants to open. Both deserve more space than you've been giving them.

One Aligned Action This Week

Choose one from each category:

The Mourning Ritual: Choose one loss that still tugs at you. Tell one trusted person, *"I'd like to mark this somehow. Can you be with me for ten minutes?"* Decide on a small ritual together, lighting a candle, looking at one photo, reading a short passage, sitting in silence while you say out loud what changed your life. Their job is not to fix or advise. It is to witness. Close with a simple phrase: "This mattered," or "Thank you for being here with me."

The Dancing Ritual: Choose one small joy, progress, or survival you've minimized. Invite someone you trust and say, "I want to actually celebrate this for ten minutes." Put on a song that feels like hope, share a meal, or let them say out loud what they're proud of you for. If moving your body feels right, let yourself sway, clap, or actually dance in your kitchen. If not, let your face show joy without shrinking it. Let yourself be toasted.

The goal is not theatrics. It's letting your body experience grief *held* and joy *amplified*—instead of asking your solitary self to carry all of it alone.

Grief and Glory: Questions for Ritual Healing

Think about the last time you truly mourned something—not just felt sad about it, but had it witnessed by someone else. How long ago was that? What's been waiting for that kind of acknowledgment?

What would you let yourself celebrate if you weren't worried about appearing to brag or be insensitive? Who would you want in the room?

Season Summary

- ➢ Weeping is private, immediate release. Mourning is communal, ritualized meaning-making. Both are needed for grief to actually move.
- ➢ Joy can be felt alone. Dancing is shared, embodied celebration that helps joy sink in and last.
- ➢ Trying to handle life's biggest losses and joys entirely alone keeps grief stuck and joy thin.
- ➢ Performing emotions publicly without letting anyone truly close still leaves you emotionally isolated.
- ➢ Some feelings are simply too big for one heart to hold—they need witnesses, stories, and ritual.
- ➢ Mourning without ever dancing leaves you heavy and afraid to re-enter life. Dancing without ever mourning leaves you disconnected from your own depth.
- ➢ Simple rituals—candles, stories, shared meals, a song played all the way through—can transform private pain into shared healing and private joy into something that actually roots.
- ➢ There is no correct timeline. Grief and joy can both be revisited and honored again, at any age, at any stage.
- ➢ The question in this season is not *"How do I get over it?"* but *"How can I let others help me carry what hurts and celebrate what heals?"*

Season Seven:
A Time to Cast Away Stones & Time to Gather Stones

There comes a point where you realize your exhaustion is not just from what you're doing—it's from everything you're carrying. Not just tasks, but invisible weights: old grudges, outdated responsibilities, inherited expectations, stories about who you're allowed to be. You look around your inner life and find yourself crossing it like a field full of rocks—careful, tense, always half-braced for the next stumble. After a while, you stop noticing the rocks. You just assume that tired and tense is simply what movement feels like.

This is the season where you learn that not every stone deserves to be carried.

In ancient Israel, a pile of stones — a 'gal-ed' — was erected at the site of every significant covenant or turning point. Not to mark what was left behind, but to mark that something real had happened here and was worth remembering.

In the ancient world, stones were not just debris—they were materials. What you threw away and what you kept determined whether a field became a place of growth or a place of ruin. Emotionally, the same is true. There are inner stones that need to be removed so anything living can grow. And there are stones—truths, memories, values, relationships—that need to be gathered, stacked, and honored as part of your foundation.

This season teaches you how to do both.

The Weight of the Unchecked Field

Imagine your inner life as a field. Over time, things have been dropped, thrown, and left there: comments you never forgot, roles you were assigned, secrets you agreed to keep, identities you picked up just to survive. Some of these are small pebbles you barely notice. Others are boulders you've been walking around for years, pretending they're just part of the landscape.

First, you learned to navigate around them. You got good at working harder, running faster, and planning more carefully. You told yourself, "This is just how life is." But at some point, the cost shows up in your body—headaches, tight shoulders, shallow breathing.

In your mind—looping thoughts, resentment, low-grade dread. In your relationships—short tempers, emotional distance, the sense that you're never fully present anywhere.

You're not weak in feeling this. You're overloaded.

The season of casting away and gathering stones begins the moment you admit: "I cannot keep carrying all of this." Not because you're incapable—but because you're human.

Stones That Were Never Yours

Some of the heaviest stones you carry were put in your hands before you were old enough to say no.

A parent's unprocessed pain. A family rule about always being "the strong one" or "the responsible one." Cultural expectations about success, gender, faith, or money. The unspoken agreement that you will keep the peace, keep the secrets, keep the image intact—no matter the cost to yourself.

At some point, the role and the person wearing it became so fused that neither of you could tell where the obligation ended, and the human being began. So, you became the one who apologized first, even when you were the one hurt. The one who answered the phone at any hour. The one who organized, soothed, explained, translated, and minimized your own needs. You carried emotional loads that were never meant for one person, much less a child.

Those stones shaped you. They also weighed you down.
Casting away stones is not a verdict on where you came from. It's the quiet act of sorting what you consciously claim from what was simply left in your hands.

You can love where you came from and still put down what it handed you. Those two things have always been able to coexist. It means gently setting down the roles that keep you from being a whole person. You can still love where you came from without carrying everything it handed you.

The Backpack of Shoulds

Nathan came to me describing his life as "a never-ending to-do list with no point." On paper, he was successful, with a stable career, family, home, and respect in his community. Inside, he felt like he was dragging himself through every single day. *"I wake up tired,"* he said, *"and I go to bed more tired."*

As we talked, a pattern emerged. Almost every sentence he used to describe his choices started with "I should." *"I should take every overtime shift." "I should handle my parents' finances—I'm the eldest." "I should never say no when my church asks for help." "I should always be available for my kids, even if I'm falling apart."*

I asked him to imagine that every "should" was a stone in a backpack he'd been wearing since childhood. We listed them out, one by one. The list was long. Some were beautiful values he genuinely believed in—integrity, generosity, commitment. Others were pure fear and obligation: never disappoint anyone, never ask for help, never rest until everything is done.

Then I asked him: "Which of these are actually yours—chosen by your adult self—and which feel like they were strapped to you by someone else's expectations?"

There was a long silence.

"This is going to sound dramatic," he said finally, *"but about half of these don't feel like mine at all. They feel like my dad's voice, my church's fear, my family's anxiety."*

That was the beginning of Nathan's stone-casting season. He didn't quit his life and move to an island. He started small—one committee he stepped off, one sibling he asked to share the load, one work request he declined without over-explaining. Each time, the world did not end. His field got a little clearer.

The Cherokee concept of 'duyvkta' — walking in one's purpose — holds that clarity doesn't arrive all at once. It emerges step by step as you remove what was never part of the path.

There were weeks he picked the stones back up the moment he set them down, convinced the world would fall apart without him holding everything together. It didn't.

Over months, something had shifted. He still worked hard, still loved deeply, still showed up. The stones he kept were ones he would have chosen even if no one was watching. Everything else, he began to gently set down.

The Fear of Letting Go

Casting away stones sounds freeing—but the experience can be terrifying. You may find yourself asking: If I stop carrying this responsibility, who will I be? If I let go of this resentment, what will protect me? If I drop this grudge, does it mean what happened was okay? If I stop being the strong one, will everything fall apart?

There is a strange safety in familiar heaviness. The weight may hurt you, but at least you know its shape. Putting it down means facing three uncomfortable truths:

First, you are not in control of everything—and never were. Second, some people may not like the lighter, clearer version of you. Third, you will have to decide who you are without your burdens as your identity.

That last one is often the hardest. The Zen tradition speaks of 'shoshin' — beginner's mind — the radical willingness to meet yourself without the accumulated labels that tell you who you already are. It is terrifying. It is also where everything new begins. If you've been "the dependable one," "the fixer," "the caretaker," or "the one who always sacrifices," it can feel disorienting to ask: *Who am I without that?"*

But here's the deeper truth of this season: The field was always there under everything you were carrying. It was waiting for you to come back to it. You're uncovering yourself. The self that existed before all the extra weight was added. The self that can still care, still show up, still love—but from a place of freedom instead of obligation.

Taking the Inventory

Before you can clear your field, you need to see what's in it. Here are the categories most people find when they look honestly:

Relationship stones that may need casting away: Friendships built on shared complaints rather than shared growth. Professional connections that take without giving back. Family dynamics that require you to stay small. Romantic patterns that repeat without teaching you anything new.

Emotional stones that need releasing: Grudges that keep you tied to old hurt. Fears that once protected you but now only limit you. Guilt about decisions you made with the information you had at the time. Shame about who you were before you knew better.

Mental stones that weigh you down: Beliefs about your limitations that are no longer true. Stories about your identity that keep you stuck in an older version of yourself. Other people's definitions of success, happiness, and worthiness that you've been living inside without realizing it.

Not every stone on this list needs to go today. But you need to know they're there before you can decide what to do with them.

Gathering The Stones Worth Keeping

If this season were only about letting go, it would feel like endless demolition. Casting away stones clears the field—but gathering stones builds something new.

In the ancient world, gathered stones became altars, fences, foundations, and memorials. In your emotional life, gathering stones means choosing what deserves a permanent place in your story: truths you're unwilling to forget, relationships you want to nurture, practices that ground you, values you're willing to live and die by.

Maybe you gather the memory of someone who loved you well—not as nostalgia that keeps you stuck, but as proof that healthy love is possible and that you've experienced it. Maybe you gather the small, overlooked moments when you acted with courage or kindness, stacking them like stones to remind yourself who you actually are when fear isn't in charge. Maybe you gather sentences that serve as anchors: Or maybe you gather the memory of one person who saw you clearly and chose to stay — and you let that memory become evidence rather than exception. "I am not responsible for everyone's happiness." "Rest is not laziness." "I can love people and still disappoint them."

Gathering stones is also about deciding which relationships belong at the center of your emotional life. Not everyone gets a front-row seat. Some people move to the balcony—not out of spite, but because that's the distance at which the relationship can be honest and sustainable. Others move closer, because they have proven themselves safe, reciprocal, and genuinely nourishing.

Relationship stones worth gathering: People who see and encourage your authentic self. Mentors who have wisdom you want to learn. Friends who challenge you while accepting you. Communities that share your values and your vision.

Wisdom stones worth keeping: Insights earned through difficult experience. Lessons from both failure and success. Practices that bring clarity and peace. Truths that help you navigate what's coming.

Some stones are load-bearing. They belong exactly where they are — at the center of who you're becoming. The key is learning to tell the difference between what looks impressive to others and what really builds something useful for your particular life.

The Pattern That Keeps You Stuck

When you resist this season, two patterns usually emerge.

In the first, you never cast away. You keep every stone out of guilt or fear. Every expectation, every obligation, every story about yourself gets added to the pile. You tell yourself you're being loyal, humble, or responsible—but slowly your field disappears under the weight. Nothing new can grow because there's no room for it.

In the second, you cast away everything. Tired of being crushed, you swing to the opposite extreme. You drop commitments overnight, cut people off dramatically, throw away values that actually anchor you, and call it freedom. For a moment, it feels exhilarating. Then you realize you've cleared the field so completely that you don't know where to stand. There's nothing to build with and nothing to lean on.

The Tao Te Ching puts it simply: 'To the mind that is still, the whole universe surrenders.' Neither hoarding nor discarding everything produces stillness. Only discernment does.

Neither extreme is wisdom. One buries you slowly. The other leaves you with nothing to stand on. This season asks for something neither — it asks for discernment, which is harder than both and worth far more.

The Shift: From Hoarding to Curating

The shift that unlocks this season is seeing yourself not as a victim of everything life has dropped into your field, but as the curator of what stays.

The ancient Egyptians practiced 'ma'at' — a principle of balance, truth, and right order. In their afterlife mythology, the heart was weighed against a feather. Not against achievement, not against reputation — against truth. The stones worth keeping are the ones that survive that scale.

A curator walks through the collection and asks one question: does this belong here, for this purpose, at this time? The rest — however beautiful, however meaningful once — goes into storage or gets released entirely. In the same way, you can acknowledge that certain expectations, stories, or roles were part of your past without giving them permanent wall space in your present.

You begin to ask different questions: Does carrying this belief help me live the life I'm meant to live right now? Does this responsibility belong to me, or am I holding it so someone else doesn't have to grow? Is this resentment protecting me—or just keeping me tied to a story where I'm always the one who was wronged? Is this relationship a stone that builds, or a stone that buries?

Over time, your field starts to look different. There is still weight—no meaningful life is weightless. But the weight you carry is chosen, not automatic. The stones you keep are the ones that align with who you are becoming, not just who you had to be to survive.

What you're building in this season is **emotional clarity** — the ability to look honestly at what you're carrying and trace it back to its actual source. Much of what weighs you down emotionally is not yours in the way you think it is. It arrived before you had the language to question it: a parent's fear that became your caution, a family's shame that became your self-doubt, a community's rules that became your inner critic. Emotional clarity means doing the genealogy. Not a genealogy of grievances — a genealogy of origins. There's a difference between understanding where something came from and deciding whether it has to stay. When you can look at a stone you've been carrying and say with genuine honesty, "this belongs to me" or "this was handed to me before I had a choice," you gain something most people never get: the ability to put things down with integrity rather than guilt.

You're not losing yourself when you cast away stones. You're uncovering yourself.

If you only remember one thing from this season: Not every stone in your field belongs to you. Some were handed to you before you were old enough to say no. This season gives you permission to look at what you're carrying, tell the truth about where it came from, and start—slowly, deliberately—setting down what was never really yours to begin with.

Season Practice: The Stone Inventory

NAME YOUR SEASON

Choose one area of your life—your family, your work, your friendships, or your inner self-talk—and make a quiet inventory of what you're carrying there.

Stones I'm carrying in this area:

1.

2.

3.

4.

5.

Now mark each one:

- ☆ = feels chosen, aligned, life-giving
- ? = feels heavy, automatic, or fueled by fear or obligation

You are not required to throw anything away today. All you are doing is telling the truth about what's in the field.

Notice Your Mind

Look at your question-mark stones. Write down what your mind says when you imagine setting one of them down.

- "I can't put this down because..."

  ____

- "If I stop carrying this, then..."

  ____

Those sentences are the fear talking. Name them clearly so they stop running things from behind the scenes.

Notice Your Body

Pick one question-mark stone—one burden you've been carrying that may not actually be yours. Hold it in your mind for a moment. What does your body do when you picture setting it down completely? Does something loosen? Does something tighten in protest? Does a part of you go very quiet? Each response is worth sitting with. Your body's response is information worth listening to.

One Aligned Action This Week

Choose one question-mark stone and ask: "What would it look like to carry this 5% less this week?" Not "How do I drop it forever?" Just one small step toward carrying it less.

Maybe it's saying no once without over-explaining.
Maybe it's asking someone else to share a load you've always taken alone. Maybe it's simply admitting to yourself: *"I don't want this role anymore."*

That's how this season moves—not with a single dramatic heave, but with many small, honest choices that slowly transform your field from a place of constant stumbling into a place where something new, and truly yours, can finally grow.

Archaeology Questions:
What's Worth Keeping, What Must Go

Which of the stones you're carrying were handed to you before you were old enough to choose them? What would it mean to acknowledge that openly—even just to yourself?

What is one stone you want to deliberately gather and keep? One truth, relationship, or value you want to place at the center of your life on purpose? What would it look like to honor that more intentionally?

Season Summary

> Your exhaustion is not just from what you're doing, it's from everything you're carrying, much of which you never consciously chose.
> Some of the heaviest stones were placed in your hands before you were old enough to say no. Recognizing that is not blame—it's clarity.
> Casting away stones doesn't mean rejecting where you came from. It means telling the truth about which burdens are yours to bear.
> You're not losing yourself when you let go. You're uncovering the person that existed before all the extra weight was added.
> Gathering stones means choosing what belongs at the center of your story: the truths, relationships, values, and memories you want to build from.
> The shift of this season is from hoarding to curating—from carrying everything automatically to choosing consciously what stays.
> Not every stone is a burden. Some are building materials for the life you're creating.
> The question is not "How do I drop everything?" but "What am I carrying that was never really mine—and what do I actually want to keep?"

Season Eight:
A Time to Rend & A Time to Sew

There are seasons when the only honest thing left to do is tear something open. You've spent years patching, smoothing, and explaining away harm—telling yourself, "it wasn't that bad," "they meant well," "I should be over this by now." The fabric of your life looks intact from a distance, but up close you can see the strain: seams pulled tight, colors faded where you've tried to wash out what really happened. You've become so skilled at maintenance that other people genuinely can't see what it costs you to keep everything looking whole.

This is the season of rending and sewing. Rending is the courageous decision to stop pretending the fabric is fine when it is already torn. Sewing is the patient work of mending in ways that make it stronger and more honest than it was before it broke. In this season, you learn when to let things tear and when to begin the slow, careful work of stitching.

The Tear You've Been Avoiding

Think about an area of your life you avoid looking at too closely. A relationship you call "complicated." A childhood you describe as "not that bad." A belief you say you "grew out of" but still flinch around. You sense a rip under the surface. You feel it when certain topics come up, when the tone in your voice shifts, when someone else's story hits a little too close to yours.

Instead of letting that tear show, you keep tugging the fabric together. You rewrite stories to make other people look better and yourself look less hurt. You blame yourself for being "too sensitive." You insist you're fine because what happened to someone else was worse.

The problem is that unacknowledged rips don't heal—they widen. The more you pretend nothing torn, the more your life has to bend around that hidden damage. Your boundaries become strange. Your reactions feel disproportionate. Your trust is shaped less by what's happening now and more by what was never named then.

Season Eight begins the moment you stop saying *"It's nothing"* and whisper: *"Actually—something broke there."*

Rending: When the Seam Must Give

In the ancient world, tearing garments was a public way of saying: *"Something has happened that normal life cannot just absorb."* It was grief made visible. The protest made it visible. A refusal to act like everything was fine when everything was not fine.

Emotionally, rending looks like finally telling the truth about the relationship that was abusive, not just "intense." The community that used your faith against you. The family pattern that harmed you even if no one meant to. The version of yourself you performed for years just to stay safe.

Rending might be a conversation where you say, *"That wasn't okay,"* even if it happened twenty years ago. It might be writing down in plain language what was done to you—or what you did that you're still ashamed of. It might be allowing anger to exist where you've only allowed sadness, because sadness was safer and anger felt too dangerous.

From the outside, rending can look like making things worse. *"Why are you bringing this up now?"* people may ask. *"Why stir the pot?"* But from the inside, something entirely different is happening: you are refusing to spend the rest of your life wearing a garment that only looks whole because you never moved freely in it.

Tearing is not the damage. The damage has already happened. Tearing is how you stop hiding it.

When You Sew Too Soon

If you grew up in a context that prized harmony, politeness, or moving on, you likely learned to sew far too early. A rupture happened, and before you could even understand the tear, someone rushed to patch it: "They didn't mean it." "Forgive and forget." "We're not going to talk about that anymore." "At least..." is followed by reasons you shouldn't feel as hurt as you do.

Every one of those sentences was designed to protect the relationship from the truth it needed most.

So you stitched. You minimized your pain, excused the other person, and tried to be mature. The external peace returned quickly. Internally, the wound stayed raw.

This shows up later as smiling through situations that make your stomach knot. Saying *"It's fine"* while your body is clearly not fine. Feeling sudden, intense reactions to small slights because they brush against old, unhealed tears that never got to breathe.

Sewing too soon is a form of self-abandonment. You are stitching the fabric back together around a wound you never let yourself see. You call it peace. Your body calls it something else. You call it reconciliation—but it's often just re-covering.

Season Eight asks you to pause the sewing kit until the tear has been fully examined.

The Peace That Hurt

Jenna grew up being the mediator in her family. When her parents fought, she cracked jokes. When her brother exploded, she smoothed things over. As an adult, she carried that role everywhere. Her coworkers called her "the glue." Her friend group called her "the therapist."

Then a close friend betrayed her—sharing private confidences during a conflict to gain sympathy from others. When Jenna confronted her, the friend cried, apologized quickly, and said: *"Can we please just move past this? I can't lose you."*

Jenna's first impulse was to sew. *"It's okay,"* she heard herself say. *"We're good."* But as she walked away, she felt a sharp, almost physical sensation in her chest. *"Something just ripped,"* she said later.
For the first time, instead of stitching it over, she let herself sit with the tear. She journaled exactly what had happened without softening it. She named her anger, her hurt, and the pattern: *"I keep patching over betrayals because I'm scared of losing people."*

Weeks later, when her friend tried to return to normal, Jenna didn't rush to reweave the friendship. *"I forgive you,"* she said, *"but trust is torn right now. If we're going to sew this back together, it has to be a different fabric. Different habits. Different boundaries."*

They didn't talk for a while. It was painful. But over time, a smaller, more honest friendship emerged—one where Jenna no longer had to be the glue holding everyone else together.

Rending, in her case, meant letting the full extent of the tear be acknowledged. Sewing meant building something new—not pretending the old fabric was never damaged.

Sewing That Honors the Tear

Healthy sewing makes the repair part of the story. Think of visible mending, the art of stitching clothes with threads that make the repair obvious and beautiful rather than invisible. The garment doesn't go back to "like new." It becomes something honest and unique, marked by what it survived.

The Japanese art of 'kintsugi' — repairing broken pottery with gold — holds that the crack is not a flaw to be hidden. It is the place where the light gets in, and where the object's history becomes its beauty.

Emotionally, sewing might look like having a follow-up conversation after the dust settles to define new expectations and boundaries. Choosing to stay in a relationship, but with different safeguards in place. Letting both the damage and the repair be part of how you describe what happened. Practicing forgiveness as a process that includes honesty, justice, and self-respect, not just a feeling of warmth you manufacture to make peace faster.

Sometimes sewing means reconciling with another person. Sometimes it means reconciling with your own past—integrating what happened into your narrative so it's no longer a secret section you skip every time you tell your story.

Sometimes it means stitching together different parts of yourself that split during pain. Most people spend years negotiating a ceasefire between these parts. This season asks for something harder and more generous: integration. The strong one and the scared one, the angry one and the gentle one, the person who survived and the person who's learning to do more than survive.

Good sewing takes time. You pull the needle through slowly. You don't force two edges together that no longer belong. You might even decide that certain connections should not be sewn back—some tears reveal fabric that was never meant to be joined in the first place. In those cases, sewing means mending *yourself,* not the relationship.

The Pattern That Keeps You Stuck

When you resist this season, you get trapped in one of two loops.

In the first, you never rend. You keep insisting everything can be worked out without ever naming what broke. You rush to excuses: " They were stressed," "I'm probably overreacting," "It's not worth making a big deal." The fabric looks intact, but you trust it less and less. Relationships become places where you manage appearances instead of telling the truth. You become very skilled at surface peace and completely unfamiliar with anything deeper.

In the second, you rip endlessly and never sew. Once you start telling the truth, you tear everything. Every slight becomes evidence. Every disappointment becomes a reason to cut people off. You feel powerful for a while—no one will hurt you again—but over time you're left holding scraps with no cloth to wrap yourself in. The Akan proverb says: 'A spider's web is not only a trap — it is also a home.' When everything becomes a threat, you end up living in your own snare.

One pattern keeps the damage invisible. The other makes everything damaged. Neither one is repairable. This season invites a response: to discern what needs to be torn open, how far the tear should go, and when to begin the slow, respectful work of mending.

The Shift: From Hiding Damage to Honest Repair

The central shift of Season Eight is moving from "Nothing's wrong" or "Everything's ruined" to "Something tore here—now what does this fabric actually need?"

Instead of reflexively minimizing harm, you let yourself say "That hurt me" without attaching a moral verdict to your sensitivity. Instead of staying forever in the catharsis of calling everything out, you start asking: "What would healing look like here—for me, for us, or at least for my own heart?"

Rending becomes honesty. Sewing becomes stewardship. Neither one is the betrayal your mind kept insisting it was; you are taking responsibility for how your story holds together going forward. The Andean concept of 'ayni' — sacred reciprocity — holds that what you give to the healing of your own life returns to everyone connected to you. Your repair is never only personal.

You begin to trust that your life can carry visible seams and still be beautiful. That you don't have to erase what happened to have a future. That your wholeness will not look like untouched perfection—it will look like fabric that has been torn, examined, and carefully mended by someone who decided it was worth keeping.

What you're building in this season is **emotional honesty** — the uncommon ability to look at damage clearly, without the two distortions that usually derail us: minimizing (pretending it's fine when it isn't) or catastrophizing (treating every tear as proof of irreparable ruin). Emotional honesty occupies the narrow, uncomfortable space in between. It says: "Something tore here. I can see it. I'm not pretending it didn't happen, and I'm not treating it as evidence that nothing can be repaired." This kind of honesty is harder than it sounds because it removes both escape routes. Most people choose one exit or the other so automatically they don't realize they've been avoiding the room entirely. The one where you don't have to feel the weight of what happened, and the one where you don't have to do the slow, unglamorous work of repair. What remains when both exits are closed is the truth: this mattered, it was damaged, and now I have to decide what an honest response looks like.

You don't have to erase what happened to have a future. You just have to stop pretending the tear isn't there—and start treating your heart with the same care you'd give to something precious and worn that you intend to keep.

If you only remember one thing from this season: Tearing is not the damage—the damage already happened. Tearing is how you stop hiding it. And sewing too soon, before the tear has been fully seen and named, is not healing. It is just re-covering. Your wholeness will not look like something untouched. It will look like something honestly mended—and that is more beautiful than pretending nothing ever broke.

Season Practice: Naming the Tear, Choosing the Stitch

Name Your Season

Choose one situation where you suspect something tore—a relationship, a community, a season of your past, or the way you see yourself. Answer these honestly:

What is the tear I've been avoiding looking at directly?
Have I been sewing too soon, or ripping without mending? Which is my default pattern?

Notice Your Mind

Write down what your mind says when you imagine letting this tear be fully seen:

- "I can't rend this because..."

- "I can't start sewing because..."

Those sentences reveal what's keeping you in the pattern. Name them so they stop running things from the shadows.

Notice Your Body

Think about the tear you named. Where does your body brace when you get close to it — your breath, your shoulders, the space behind your eyes? Now think about what it would feel like to say, clearly and without softening: 'Something broke there.' Does something loosen or lock? That response has been waiting longer than you know.

One Aligned Action This Week

Choose one step—either deeper into honest rending, or one step toward gentle sewing. Not both at once.

If rending: Write down in plain language—no softening, no qualifiers—what happened. Let the sentence be blunt: "When ___ happened, something in me broke." Write it privately, just for you. That's enough for now.

If sewing: Ask yourself what mending *you* looks like—not the relationship, just you. Maybe it's scheduling a therapy session. Writing a letter you don't send. Setting one new boundary. Telling one trusted person the full, unsoftened story for the first time.

Fabric of Your Life Questions: Repair or Release?

Where have you been sewing too soon rushing to forgive, reconcile, or move on before the tear was fully named? What would it mean to go back and let yourself see it clearly?

Think of one relationship or situation where visible mending—repair that doesn't pretend the damage never happened—might be possible. What would the first honest stitch look like?

Season Summary

- Rending is naming and exposing tears that already exist; it is honesty, not new harm.
- Sewing is mending that honors the tear instead of hiding it. Good repair integrates the wound into your story rather than erasing it.
- Minimizing damage, "It wasn't that bad"—keeps you wearing lives and relationships that can't truly hold you.
- Sewing too soon—rushing to forgive, reconcile, or move on— often means abandoning your own pain before it's had a chance to be seen.
- Endless ripping without sewing leads to isolation. You're protected but uncovered.
- Visible seams are signs of strength and wisdom, not failure. They show where you chose truth over appearance.
- Sometimes sewing means rebuilding a relationship. Sometimes it means stitching *yourself* back together and letting the relationship go.
- You don't need to erase what happened to have a future. You need to integrate it so it no longer secretly controls you.
- The question in this season is not "How do I make this look untouched?" but "How do I tell the truth about where it tore— and choose repairs that let me live honestly?"

MOVEMENT FOUR:
RELATIONAL & MORAL WISDOM
How You Speak, Love, Fight, and Make Peace

You've done the harder half of the work already. You've faced what needed to end, cleared what was overdue, built something that fits, and started telling the truth about your own inner weather. Now life hands you the part you can't do alone. You've let some things die so others could be born, uprooted what was draining you, dismantled structures that couldn't hold you, and started building a life that fits who you are becoming. You've also become more fluent in your own emotional weather, allowing tears and laughter, mourning and dancing, clearing what no longer belongs, and carefully mending what does.

Now comes the question you cannot avoid forever: What does all this mean for how you live with other people?

Ecclesiastes understood that the hardest work of a human life is not internal — it is relational. The pairings that govern how we speak, love, fight, and make peace take up more of the book than any other category. The ancient writer knew where people most often lose the thread of their own wisdom."

It's one thing to find your truth in a journal or a therapist's office. It's another to bring that truth into conversations, conflicts, commitments, and daily interactions without either collapsing or bulldozing.

Movement Four is where your inner seasons and your outer life meet in the space between you and others.

Why This Movement Matters

Most of our deepest regrets live in this territory.

Words we didn't say when someone needed to hear them. Words we did say that we can't take back. Love we gave without any boundaries— and love we withheld where safety was possible. Fights we avoided until resentment hardened into stone, or battles we escalated into wars that didn't need to be fought. Embraces we offered too easily to people who hadn't earned them, and ones we refused when someone had genuinely changed.

All the inner clarity in the world still must pass through your mouth, your choices, and your presence before it becomes anything real in another person's life. If you don't know when to keep silent and when to speak, when to love and when to hate, when to go to war and when to make peace, when to embrace and when to step back. This Movement exists to give you a framework for those hardest calls—not a script, but a compass.

The ability to read what a moment needs — whether it calls for truth or silence, engagement or release, closeness or distance — and then act from that reading rather than from habit or fear, is the whole game. Every season in this Movement is a different version of that same skill applied to a different relational context.

The Four Axes of Relational Wisdom

Ecclesiastes names four pairings that together describe the core tensions of living well with other people:

A time to keep silence, and a time to speak. A time to love, and a time to hate. A time of war, and a time of peace. A time to embrace, and a time to refrain from embracing.

These four pairings are the daily questions running beneath every significant relationship you have. They don't announce themselves. They just shape every conversation you've ever had without knowing their names. Do I say this, or let it go? Do I keep offering my heart here, or pull back? Is this a situation to confront, or one to release? Has this person earned closeness, or is distance the most honest thing I can offer right now?

In Movement Four, each season takes one of these axes and turns it into practical discernment—so that your inner transformation doesn't stay trapped inside you but finally shapes the way you move through the world.

The Cost of Getting This Wrong

When you don't understand these relational seasons, you tend to default to one of two survival strategies.

In the first, you make everything about peace and love. You avoid hard truths to keep the atmosphere calm. You love people by abandoning yourself. You never declare war on patterns that are destroying you because you're terrified of conflict. You embrace too quickly, stay too long, and confuse niceness with goodness.

In the second, you make everything about war and truth. You say whatever you think whenever you think it and call it honesty. You live in constant battle mode, reading every disagreement as a fight to be won. You withhold embrace to stay safe but end up lonely.

Both are forms of self-protection that became self-imprisonment. The difference between them is smaller than it feels from the inside. Both strategies were smart once. They kept you safe in environments where genuine relational wisdom wasn't modeled or available. They just can't take you where you want to go.

From Inner Alignment to Outer Integrity

The work you've done in earlier movements was not theoretical. It was preparation.

In Movement One, you learned that everything has seasons—that beginnings and endings, planting and uprooting, are built into the rhythm of life. In Movement Two, you learned to protect yourself—to end what is killing you, to dismantle what doesn't fit, to build structures that can hold you. In Movement Three, you became more honest with your own heart—letting grief and joy coexist, clearing what doesn't belong, tearing and mending with intention.

None of that work was practice. It was the real thing. And it prepared you for this.

Movement Four is where all of that becomes visible in your choices with others. Speaking a hard truth is a very different thing when you've already done your own emotional work than when you're using truth as a weapon. The Sufi poet Hafiz wrote that even after all this time the sun never says to the earth 'You owe me.' That is what love seasoned by wisdom looks like in practice — giving without accounting, truth without weaponizing, presence without demand.

Choosing distance lands differently when it flows from clarity and care than when it flows from unprocessed fear. Going to war with a pattern that's harming you changes entirely when you've already dealt with your own self-sabotage rather than projecting your pain outward.

Awareness changes what you're responsible for. Not the old crushing obligation to keep everyone comfortable — but the responsibility to align your speech, your love, your fights, and your embraces with what is true. You are not responsible for other people's reactions. You *are* responsible for whether you spoke when it was time to speak, stayed silent when silence was needed, loved what is good, refused to cooperate with what is destructive, fought the battles that were yours, and opened your arms where it was wise. This is the standard that has been applied to human beings in every wisdom tradition that has ever thought carefully about how people should treat each other.

You will not get this perfect. No one does. But you can grow from default reactions to deliberate responses—from people-pleasing or constant combat to something far more grounded. Relational wisdom that matches the person you're becoming — and is finally worthy of the people who deserve the best of you.

Season Nine:
A Time to Keep Silence & A Time to Speak

There are seasons when the hardest part of your life is not what you feel—it's what you do, or don't do, with your voice. You replay conversations in your head, rewriting what you wish you'd said or unsaying words you regret. You stay quiet when something in you is screaming to speak, or you've simply been quiet for so long that you're not entirely sure anymore what you think. Or you speak in ways that leave a wake you didn't intend.

This is the season of silence and speech. A wiser rhythm where silence becomes an act of love and speech becomes an act of courage — and both become forms of self-respect. Every sentence you say, or swallow is either building something or eroding something—inside you, between you and another person, or in the spaces around you.

The Conversation That Won't Let You Go

Think about the interaction that still lives rent-free in your mind. The moment you knew you should have said no and didn't. The time you laughed something off that hurt. The meeting where you stayed silent while someone was treated unfairly. Or the argument where you unleashed all the unsaid things from the last five years in one volcanic monologue.

Ecclesiastes observed it plainly: there is a time to keep silence and a time to speak. The wisdom was never in choosing one over the other forever — it was in knowing which moment you were standing in.

In each of those scenes, the question underneath was simple: Was this a time to keep silent, or a time to speak?

We rarely pause there in real time. We default to our training. Some of us were raised to keep the peace at any cost, so silence feels safer than truth. Others were raised to never let anyone disrespect you, so we speak quickly, sharply, and often calling it honesty. Season Nine invites you to break those automatic patterns and find a third way.

How You Learned to Use—or Hide—Your Voice

Your relationship with silence and speech didn't start yesterday. It was shaped in rooms you barely remember.

If you grew up in a home where emotions or opinions were punished, you learned that silence is safety. You kept your worries to yourself, told adults what they wanted to hear, and became skilled at reading the room instead of expressing yourself. Reading the room is a gift. Losing yourself in it is the cost nobody warns you about. As an adult, you may find yourself editing your thoughts mid-sentence to avoid conflict, saying "I'm fine" by reflex, or thinking of the perfect response hours later when you're alone.

If you grew up in a loud home—where shouting was normal, boundaries were blurry, and whoever spoke the strongest won—you may have learned that volume equals power. As an adult, you might talk over quieter people without realizing it, say it like it is and then feel confused when others pull away, or use truth as a shield or a sword instead of a bridge.

Neither pattern is a character flaw. They are survival strategies. They are the intelligence of a younger self doing what it took to stay safe. But the tactics that kept you protected then have a way of keeping you isolated now. If left unchecked, it slowly becomes the reason your relationships feel flat, tense, or volatile. Season Nine is where you learn a third way: silence and speech as tools, not reflexes. The Quaker tradition calls it 'speaking truth to power' — but in its original form, it began much quieter than that: with learning to speak truth to yourself first, and then outward from that center.

When Silence Heals, and When It Harms

Silence can be holy. It can also be harmful. Silence heals when you pause to listen rather than reacting from heat. When you keep someone's vulnerability in confidence instead of turning it into a story. When you abstain from speaking in spaces where your voice would center you instead of those who are directly impacted.

When you decide not to correct every small inaccuracy because the relationship matters more than being right. In those moments, silence is an act of respect—for yourself, for the other person, for the moment. It creates space for reflection, de-escalation, or someone else's voice to finally be heard.

The Desert Fathers of early Christianity called this 'hesychia' — a sacred stillness that was not emptiness but the fullest possible attention. Silence, practiced well, is presence at its most concentrated.

Silence harms when you swallow truths that are needed for growth because you're afraid of conflict. When you let harmful comments slide in front of people who are being diminished by them. When you pretend you agree while secretly resenting the person, you just quietly accommodate. When you say nothing about a boundary that's been crossed—and then punish the other person in your head for weeks. In those moments, silence becomes complicity with your own discomfort. You keep the peace on the outside by making war inside yourself. The work of this season is learning to ask, in real time: Is my silence protecting something worth protecting—or betraying it?

When Speech Liberates, and When It Wounds

Speech can be medicine. It can also be a weapon. Speech liberates when you name a boundary clearly and calmly: "I'm not available for that." When you tell the truth about how something affected you without turning it into a verdict on the other person's character. When you speak up for someone who has less power in the room. The ability to feel what the room needs — not just what you need — is one of the quietest forms of strength there is. When you finally say the affirming, encouraging, or grateful words you've been keeping in your head. In those moments, words become bridges. They clarify reality, invite repair, or nurture what is good.

The Talmud teaches that the tongue has no bones — it can move in any direction. Which is precisely why every tradition that has ever thought carefully about human community has also thought carefully about when to use it.

Speech wounds when you use "honesty" as an excuse to unload everything you feel in the harshest way possible. When you share someone else's story without their consent. When you win the argument but lose trust because your tone told the other person they were an opponent, not a partner. When you talk so much there's no room for anyone else's experience to exist.

Sometimes the problem isn't that you spoke, it's how and when you did. A true sentence delivered at the wrong time, in the wrong spirit, to the wrong person, can do real damage even when the content is accurate.

And the other side matters just as much: not speaking can also wound. The apology you never gave. The *"I love you"* you assumed they already knew. The *"I believe you"* you stayed quiet about because you didn't want to get involved. Season Nine has one ask: "Do you mean what you say, and say what you mean, at a time and in a way that serves the moment.

The Email She Didn't Send

Leah drafted a long email to her manager at 2 a.m. It was sharp, detailed, and—if she was being honest—accurate. Her manager had been taking credit for her work, dismissing her ideas in meetings, then quietly implementing them later. Leah was furious.

Her first impulse was to hit send. *"I'm done staying quiet,"* she thought. *"I'm over being the nice one."*

Instead, she slept on it. In the morning, she read the email again and asked herself two questions: *"What here is true and important?"* and *"What here is just me wanting to hurt back?"*

She deleted the second category. The remaining email was shorter, calmer, and clearer. She requested a meeting instead of firing off a monologue. In the meeting, she named specific behaviors, explained how they impacted her work, and stated clearly what she needed to see going forward.

Her manager was defensive at first, then unsettled, then quiet. Over the next few weeks, her behavior began to shift. Leah hadn't stayed silent. She also hadn't used her words to burn the entire bridge. She had chosen a *time to speak* that honored both her dignity and her goals. She didn't win the argument. She changed the dynamic. Those are not the same thing, and the second one lasts longer.

That is the kind of discernment this season is building in you.

The Pattern That Keeps You Stuck

When you resist this season, you bounce between two exhausting extremes.

In one pattern, you under-speak. You tell yourself, "It's not worth it," "They won't listen anyway," "I don't want to cause drama." You stay quiet and hope people will just know what you need or how you feel. They rarely do. Resentment builds. You start distancing without ever having given the relationship a chance to meet you in truth.

The Sioux concept of 'mitákuye oyás'iŋ' — all things are related — carries a quiet warning: what you withhold from one relationship eventually shapes every relationship. Silence that starts as self-protection rarely stays contained.

In the other pattern, you overspeak. You hold everything in until your breaking point, then say too much, too harshly, all at once. Or you narrate every frustration as it happens, so people feel constantly criticized even when you're not wrong. Your words become noise rather than guidance.

Either way, what you wanted was to be truly heard. Neither pattern gets you there. Both keep you from the intimacy you want. The shift in this season is from *impulse* to *intent*.

The Shift: From Automatic to Aligned

The core shift of Season Nine is simple to state and lifelong to practice: you stop using silence and speech as reflexes and start using them as choices. That gap between what you feel and what you do with it — even when it's only three seconds wide — is where your character actually lives.

Before you respond, you begin to ask: What am I trying to protect right now—my comfort, or what's truly important? If I stay silent, what grows here? If I speak, what grows here? Is this the right person, right time, and right setting for this truth?

You start to see silence as one of your tools, not your only safety. You start to see speech as a form of stewardship, each word an investment in the kind of relationship and world you want to live in. Every conversation is either a deposit or a withdrawal. The account you build over time is called trust.

The Buddhist concept of 'samma vaca' — right speech — was one of the eight paths to liberation. Not because words are sacred in the abstract, but because every word either moves you toward the life you want or away from it.

Over time, people experience you differently. You become someone who's quiet the room can feel — not as absence, but as a kind of held attention. Someone whose words carry weight precisely because they arrive only when they're ready.

You won't get this perfect. You will still speak too soon sometimes and stay quiet too long other times. But instead of judging yourself, you'll learn from each moment—slowly learning to feel the difference between 'this is a time to keep silent' and 'this is a time to speak' not as a rule, but as a living sense you carry with you.

What you're building in this season is **emotional self-expression** — not the volume of what you say, but the alignment between what you genuinely feel and what you choose to communicate, and when, and to whom.

Most people operate at one of two extremes: they say too little because speaking feels dangerous, or they say too much because silence feels like abandonment.

One keeps you hidden. The other empties you. Neither one is the same as actually being known. Real emotional self-expression requires that you know what you feel before you speak, that you choose words that match the truth of your experience, and that you deliver them in a way the other person can receive. That kind of care — choosing words not just for what they express but for what they can build — is one of the rarest things one person can offer another. It is a skill that requires you to slow down between stimulus and response — not to suppress what's real, but to give it the form that actually serves the relationship and honors what is true.

Every sentence you say or swallow is either building something or eroding something. The question is whether you're choosing consciously—or just reacting.

If you only remember one thing from this season: Silence and speech are both forms of power—and both can be used to protect life or betray it. The goal is not to talk more or less. It's to pause long enough to ask what your silence or your words will actually grow—and then choose that, on purpose.

Season Practice: The 3-Breath Check-In

Name Your Season

Think of two recent situations—one where you stayed silent and wished you'd spoken, and one where you spoke and wished you'd stayed quiet.

A time I stayed silent when I should have spoken:

What it cost me or the relationship:

A time I spoke when silence would have served better:

What it cost me or the relationship:

Notice Your Mind

Write down your default reflex—the pattern you fall into without thinking:

- My reflex when things feel tense is to...

- The story I tell myself to justify that reflex is...

Naming your default loosens its grip on you.

Notice Your Body

Think about a current situation where you're unsure whether to speak or stay quiet. Notice what your body does in the pause — does your breath hold, does something in you lean forward or pull back, does a part of you go very still? Now imagine speaking clearly and calmly. Now imagine staying quiet with full intention rather than fear. Your body will respond differently to each. That difference is information.

One Aligned Action This Week

Next time you feel the urge to either blurt something out or shut down completely, try this before you respond:

Three slow breaths. While you breathe, ask silently: "Am I trying to avoid discomfort, prove a point, or serve what actually matters here?"

Then choose one aligned micro-move:

If your reflex is silence: add one small sentence of truth. "I actually see that differently." Or: "That comment stung, and I want you to know why."

If your reflex is over-speaking: add one small sentence of restraint. "I need a moment to think about how to say this." Or: "Can we come back to this when I'm less charged?"

Voice and Stillness: Questions for the Communicator Within

Where in your life right now are you staying silent when something in you knows it's time to speak? What's the one sentence you've been swallowing?

Where are you over-speaking—using words to manage your anxiety, fill the space, or control the outcome? What would one moment of intentional quiet make possible?

Season Summary

- Your patterns with silence and speech were learned early. They are survival strategies, not moral verdicts.
- Silence can protect and honor—but it can also become complicity and self-betrayal.
- Speech can liberate and heal—but it can also wound when driven by reactivity rather than intent.
- Under-speaking breeds resentment and distance. Over-speaking breeds defensiveness and noise.
- Some truths need timing, setting, and a prepared heart to land well. Honesty without wisdom can still cause harm.
- Not speaking can hurt too—the apology never given, the affirmation never voiced, the injustice never named.
- The question shifts from *"Do I talk or stay quiet?"* to *"What will my silence or my speech grow here?"*
- A brief pause—three breaths—between feeling and response can change entire conversations.
- The goal is not perfect communication but aligned communication: using your voice and your quiet to serve what is true and life-giving, for you and for the people you're walking with.

Season Ten:
A Time to Love & A Time to Hate

There are seasons when the question is no longer "Do I care?" but "What am I willing to care about and what am I no longer willing to care for at the cost of myself?" You feel the split inside you: one part wants to keep loving, understanding, and empathizing, while another part is quietly sick of excusing what keeps harming you. That internal argument has probably been running longer than you realize — and it is costing you more energy than either side is worth. You're tired of calling it compassion when you abandon yourself, and tired of calling it strength when you harden your heart against everything.

This is the season of love and hate. Sentimental love says yes to everything and slowly disappears inside its own generosity. Destructive hate burns the house down and calls it justice. This season is looking for something more honest than either. Here you learn what it means to aim your love at what is genuinely life-giving, and to turn your hate—your deep, clear *no*—toward what destroys life, dignity, and truth in you and around you.

When "Love" Has Been Used Against You

For many of us, love was first defined as pleasing, accommodating, and staying. You were praised for being "so loving" when you let people cross your boundaries without consequence, kept forgiving behavior that never changed, and took responsibility for other people's feelings. You were encouraged to stay loyal to roles that were quietly draining you—and if you questioned any of them, someone had a verse, a slogan, or a guilt-soaked reminder ready.

Ecclesiastes is unsparing on this point: there is a time to love and a time to hate. Not as moral failure — as seasonal wisdom. The same book that commands love also makes room for refusal.

You learned to stretch your love until it became impossible to tell where you ended and everyone else's needs began. You called it faithfulness when, in truth, it was fear—fear of being alone, of being called selfish, of being labeled unloving. At some point, often after a sleepless night or a breaking moment, another question finally surfaces: If this is what love is, why does it feel like slow death?

Season Ten begins when you stop trying to fix that feeling and start listening to it. Something in you has recognized that your definition of love has been hijacked. You have been training your heart to stay loyal to what keeps you small. Noticing that pattern — really noticing it, without immediately defending it — is one of the most disorienting and necessary things a person can do.

Reclaiming Hate: What You Refuse to Cooperate With

The word "hate" has probably felt off-limits to you. You associate it with prejudice, cruelty, or hard-heartedness—so you avoid it entirely. In doing so, you also avoid one of the most important movements of a healthy soul: refusing to cooperate with what harms.

The hate this season is asking about has one target: what disfigures people — cruelty, exploitation, manipulation, degradation, and the patterns that keep you small, silent, or ashamed. It is about refusing to tolerate what disfigures them—cruelty, exploitation, manipulation, degradation, and the patterns that keep you small, silent, or ashamed. To hate in this sense is to say a clear inner *no* to abuse, to manipulation, to the parts of yourself that lie in order to survive, and to the systems you quietly benefit from that crush others while you stay neutral.

Every tradition that has ever thought seriously about love has also thought seriously about what love refuses. The Hebrew prophets named it 'sin'at ra' — hatred of evil — and considered it inseparable from the love of what is good. The two were never meant to exist without each other. The two have never been separated. Love without the capacity for hate becomes mushy, enabling. Hate without love becomes ruthless destruction. You were made for both—a fierce yes and a holy no.

The Love That Was Killing Her

Elena had been with Mark for seven years. Everyone around them said things like, *"You two are amazing together—you've been through so much,"* and they weren't entirely wrong. What no one really saw was how they had been through it: Elena doing most of the emotional labor, absorbing outbursts, forgiving repeated betrayals, and constantly shrinking her needs to keep the peace.

"I know he's broken," she told me. *"I know his childhood was rough. How can I walk away from that? Love doesn't give up, right?"* Her voice shook most on the word "love," as if she were reciting a script she didn't fully believe anymore.

Instead of asking whether she loved him enough, we explored something else: "What if love doesn't mean you have to be the one who breaks to keep him company?" For the first time, she put words to both sides of what she felt.

On one page, she wrote what she genuinely appreciated about Mark— his creativity, his humor, his tenderness on his good days. On another, she wrote what she hated about what happened to her in the relationship, how small she felt, how often she apologized for his behavior, how she had quietly stopped seeing friends he didn't like, how her body had begun whispering through migraines and anxiety. When she looked at both pages together, she went quiet. *"I think I've been loving him and hating myself,"* she said.

Some sentences take years to arrive. That one had been waiting in her for a long time.

That realization was the doorway into this season. She didn't suddenly stop caring about him. She redirected her deepest loyalty: *"I will not keep sacrificing my health, sanity, and future on the altar of his unresolved pain. I can love him and still refuse to cooperate with what is destroying both of us."*

Leaving didn't happen overnight. But the inner shift came first. Her hate finally had a worthy target—not Mark as a person, but the dynamics that refused to change. Once that became clear, her actions slowly began to match.

The Pattern: Loving What Hurts, Hating What Heals

When you resist this season, you often get the axis completely backwards. You end up loving what is familiar, even when it's corrosive—and hating what would actually heal you because it feels scary, unfamiliar, or selfish.

You might love your overwork because it makes you feel needed and important, and hate rest because it exposes your emptiness. You might cling to a relationship that keeps you anxious because the intensity feels like proof that it's real—and quietly avoid the quiet, sturdy friendships that don't give you the same adrenaline.

You might adore your image as the selfless one and secretly despise boundaries, direct asks, or saying no.

Underneath all of this, your nervous system has confused love with adrenaline, drama, and self-erasure. Somewhere along the way, your nervous system learned that caring for yourself was the same as abandoning others. That is a lie worth examining.

The Stoics called this 'phantasia kataleptike' — the accurate impression, the seeing of things as they actually are, rather than as habit or fear has taught you to see them. Most of us are working from old impressions that have never been updated.

In this season, you begin retraining your instincts. Love moves you toward what sustains life. Hate moves you away from what slowly kills it.

When Loving Means Letting Go

There comes a point where the most loving thing you can do is stop cushioning the impact of reality. This does not mean abandoning people in their hours of need or withdrawing the moment something gets difficult. It means refusing to keep absorbing the consequences of someone else's refusal to grow. Feeling what someone else feels is a gift. Feeling it instead of them, so they never have to have to — that is where empathy quietly becomes a trap.

Sometimes the most loving action is to end a relationship you have been resuscitating alone. Sometimes it is to step out of a church, workplace, or community that will not acknowledge harm, no matter how many private conversations you've had. Sometimes it is to stop covering for someone's addiction, unreliability, or cruelty—and to let the truth of their choices land where it belongs.

People watching may call it hardness. People who've lived inside the quiet relief of finally stopping know it as mercy — mostly toward yourself. The Buddhist concept of 'upekkha' — equanimity, the capacity to love without attachment to outcome — holds that the highest form of care sometimes looks like release. Not abandonment. Release. Love that never says "enough" is not love. It is captivity with a pretty name.

When Hate Becomes a Teacher

In this season, hate is not rage without reason. It is a bright, clarifying signal: *something here is against my soul.* Instead of shaming yourself for the intensity of your no, you become curious about it.

Notice where you can't stand yourself or your circumstances anymore, the way you turn on yourself every time something goes wrong, the way you shrink in certain rooms, the way you talk to your body, your younger self, or your creativity. Rather than pushing that disgust away, ask: "What is this revulsion trying to defend in me?" The ability to stay curious about your own intensity — rather than acting it out or shutting it down — is one of the rarest and most useful things you can develop.

Often, hate shows up as a fierce protector of your dignity, your calling, and your integrity. "I can't keep letting them talk to me like that" is hate defending dignity. "I hate how I disappear into everyone else's priorities" is hate defending your calling. "I hate lying about who I am to stay accepted" is hate defending your integrity.

In those moments, hate is pointing you back to love: "This is not worthy of you. Choose differently." The Yoruba concept of 'iwa pele' — gentle character, the alignment between inner truth and outer action — suggests that when you feel strong revulsion at something in your life, it is often your deepest character refusing to be betrayed.

The Shift: From Unconditional Yes to Discerned Love

The core shift of Season Ten is moving from indiscriminate love and reactive hate to discerned affection and intentional refusal. You stop asking "Am I loving enough?" and begin asking "What, exactly, am I loving here—and is it truly worthy of my heart?"

You start to distinguish between loving a person's humanity and loving the pattern that keeps you both stuck. You can hold compassion for someone's history while refusing to keep participating in their harm. That distinction — between caring about a person and endorsing a dynamic — is where mature love lives. You can recognize the beauty in a community's intentions while refusing to ignore the damage of its practices.

Love, in this season, looks like staying when growth is mutual—even if it's messy—and leaving when staying only sustains denial. It looks like investing in relationships, work, and practices that nourish your aliveness, and extending compassion without letting it become self-erasure.

Hate, in this season, looks like saying *"never again"* to cycles of abuse, manipulation, or internal self-attack. It looks like taking your hands off outcomes you have been trying to control and putting your energy where it can take root in something real.

The invitation of this season is precision — not coldness. A heart that knows what it's saying yes to and means it. Someone whose love is deep and discerning, whose no is as sacred as their yes.

The Desert Mothers of early Christianity — the 'ammas' — taught that the soul's deepest work is learning to distinguish between what feeds it and what flatters it. Love that feeds you will sometimes ask hard things. Love that only flatters you will eventually hollow you out.

What you're building in this season is **emotional aim** — the capacity to direct your love and your refusals toward what is worthy of them, rather than dispersing both indiscriminately based on habit, fear, or who is most demanding. Your emotional energy is not infinite.

The love you pour into what is actively harming you is love unavailable to what is quietly deserving it. The resentment you direct at safe people is energy that belongs in the places where you've been genuinely wronged. Emotional aim is not coldness — it is precision. It is the decision to stop giving your most generous self to situations that have proven they cannot receive it, and to stop withholding your tenderness from people who have earned it. When your love and your refusals are aimed at each other well, they stop canceling each other out and start building something coherent.

Love without the capacity for hate becomes mushy enabling. Hate without love becomes ruthless destruction. You were made for both—a fierce yes and a holy no.

If you only remember one thing from this season: You are not losing your tenderness in this season—you are giving it better aim. Your love stops funding your own destruction. Your hate becomes a guardian of the life you are finally willing to live. A discerning no is not the opposite of love. It is one of love's most courageous expressions.

Season Practice: Your Love/Hate Inventory

Name Your Season

Set aside a quiet moment and a blank page. Make two lists:

I am currently loving (people, roles, habits, environments I pour
energy into):

1.

2.

3.

4.

I am currently hating (situations, patterns, behaviors—inside me or
around me—that I most strongly resent or resist):

1.

2.

3.

4.

Notice Your Mind

For each item on your "loving" list, ask: *"Does this genuinely give life—to me, to them, to the relationship—or am I calling it love while it slowly empties me?"*

For each item on your "hating" list, ask: *"Is this something genuinely harmful that deserves my refusal—or have I been trained to hate something that would actually heal me, like rest, boundaries, therapy, or vulnerability?"*

Write down what you notice. The answers that surprise you are usually the most important.

Notice Your Body

Think about one thing on your loving list that may be costing you more than it gives. Does your body feel heavier when you think about continuing it — a kind of bracing, a held breath, a subtle flattening? Now think about something on your hating list that might actually be healthy for you. Where does your body soften toward it, even slightly, even against your will? That softening is information your mind hasn't caught up to yet.

One Aligned Action This Week

Choose one place where your love and hate need to trade targets:

Maybe you begin to love what you were taught to hate—your limits, your need for help, your quiet strengths, your right to rest.

Maybe you finally refuse what you were pressured to love—a role that crushes you, a dynamic that never changes, an inner critic you've been treating like truth.

Take one concrete action this week that reflects that shift: a boundary you set, a conversation you have, an obligation you release, or a private declaration you write down and keep somewhere you'll see it.

Heart Inventory:
Questions for Conscious Emotional Investment

Where in your life are you calling something love when it is actually fear—fear of being alone, of disappointing someone, of being labeled unloving? What would honest love look like in that same situation?

What is one thing your hate has been trying to protect in you that you've been ignoring or shaming? What would it mean to listen to that signal instead of silencing it?

Season Summary

> Love was likely first defined for you as pleasing, accommodating, and staying—regardless of the cost to yourself.
> When love becomes indistinguishable from self-abandonment, it stops being love. It becomes captivity with a pretty name.
> Hate, rightly understood, is not cruelty, it is the refusal to cooperate with what destroys life, dignity, and truth.
> Love without the capacity for hate becomes enabling. Hate without love becomes destruction. You were made for both.
> When you get the axis backwards, you end up loving what is familiar and harmful—and hating what would heal you.
> The most loving thing you can do is sometimes stop cushioning the impact of someone else's choices and let truth land where it belongs.
> Hate as a teacher points you back to love: *This is not worthy of you. Choose differently.*
> The shift is from indiscriminate yes to discerned affection— from *"Am I loving enough?"* to *"Is what I'm loving actually worthy of my heart?"*
> You are not becoming colder in this season. You are becoming truer—someone whose love is deep and discerning, and whose no is as sacred as their yes.

Season Eleven:
A Time of War & A Time of Peace

There are seasons when being kind, understanding, and reasonable is no longer enough to move your life forward. You have already tried empathy. You have already tried compromise. You have already tried letting it go. And still, the same harm keeps repeating. Something in you begins to realize: if I keep avoiding this fight, I am not keeping the peace—I am keeping the problem. That distinction — between keeping the peace and keeping the problem — is the whole season in a single sentence.

This is the time of war and peace. War, in this season, is courageous engagement with what is genuinely wrong. Peace is the hard-won rest that follows refusing to fight battles that were never yours. Both require more discernment than most people realize. This is where you learn when to stand your ground and when to lay your weapons down. When to pick up the sword, and when to finally release it.

The Pattern That Keeps You in the Wrong Battles

Most of us get war and peace completely backwards. We go to war where peace would serve us, and we make peace where we should be at war.

You might avoid necessary conflict with the people who are harming you, while fighting constantly with people who are safe. You swallow your truth with a partner who crosses your boundaries, then argue fiercely with a friend over something small because that feels like a safer place to have a fight. You stay silent at work when something unethical happens, then go home and fight about the dishes because that's a conflict you know how to have.

On the other hand, you may be waging a private war against yourself while trying to keep the outside world calm. You attack your body in the mirror, your decisions in your head, your past in your memory. You are relentless with yourself and excessively peaceful with everyone else. You bleed for other people's comfort while refusing to confront what is slowly killing you.

When you resist this season, you either live in constant low-grade conflict—always on edge, always defending, always bracing—or in fragile, surface-level peace that depends on you never saying what you really think. In both cases, you are exhausted. You are fighting the wrong enemies with the wrong weapons at the wrong time.

Sun Tzu observed it twenty-five centuries ago: the supreme art of war is to subdue the enemy without fighting. The battles that cost you the most are rarely the ones that need to happen at all.

What War Really Means in a Soul

War, in this season, is not about destroying people. It is about confronting patterns, agreements, and systems that cannot be made safe by kindness alone. War is any intentional move to stop harm when pretending, explaining, or accommodating has failed.

War can look like finally saying no and sticking to it. The gap between the moment you feel the urge to fight and the moment you decide how — that pause is where wisdom either shows up or doesn't. Like naming reality in a room that has survived on denial. Like leaving a job, relationship, or community that will not change no matter how much you contort yourself. Like filing the report, calling the meeting, setting the boundary, or walking away.

Inwardly, war might mean refusing to keep cooperating with an inner voice that calls you worthless. It might mean dismantling beliefs that say you deserve mistreatment or that your needs are an inconvenience. It might mean choosing—repeatedly—to act from your values instead of your fears.

War is your courage to decide that truth, safety, dignity, and the protection of those who cannot protect themselves matter more than your comfort in this moment.

Ecclesiastes holds both in the same breath: a time of war and a time of peace — not as a contradiction, but as the full range of what a faithful life requires. Refusing either one is refusing half of what you were made for.

The Battles in Your Life Right Now

To navigate this season, it helps to distinguish between three kinds of battles you may be carrying.

Battles that are yours to fight. These are places where your voice, your action, or your boundary is clearly needed—a relationship where you have been avoiding hard truth, a workplace pattern you are uniquely positioned to challenge, an internal battle with addiction, self-hatred, or perfectionism that only you can confront.

Battles that are not yours alone. These are conflicts that require shared responsibility—a marriage that needs counseling, a team dynamic that needs collective change, a family pattern that needs more than one person's courage. Your part matters, but you cannot win these alone. Your war here is to stop being the only one in the room willing to name what everyone already knows — and insist that others carry their weight. Sometimes the partnership you need is not with another person — it is with a therapist, a community, or a tradition wiser than your current moment.

Battles that are not yours at all. These are fights you wander into because you are uncomfortable with other people's discomfort or silence. You referee everyone's relationships, absorb everyone's crises, and become emotionally invested in conflicts that do not belong to you. In this category, fighting is actually a form of avoidance—you wage wars on other people's fronts, so you don't have to face your own.

The ability to read which kind of battle you're in — yours, shared, or borrowed — is one of the most underrated skills a person can develop. Most people make this assessment based on emotion alone. This season asks you to make it based on evidence.

Wisdom in this season means placing each battle in its proper category. You stop abandoning the battles only you can fight. You stop fighting alone where you need partnership. And you stop waging wars that were never your assignment.

The Season That Wrote This Book

There is a particular kind of season that arrives without asking permission — the one where several enormous things happen at once, and none of them will wait for the others to finish. I know that season from the inside.

My mother was gone. The business I had believed in enough to bet my stability on was still too young to stand on its own. And the woman I loved — genuinely loved, not the way people use that word casually — was no longer in my life, because the honest version of me and the honest version of that relationship could not occupy the same future.

Three losses dressed in different clothes. One looked like grief. One looked like courage. One looked like failure, at least from the outside. And some days, all three looked exactly the same.

What nobody tells you about a season like that is how disorienting it is to fight and grieve and begin all at once. I couldn't finish mourning my mother before the business demanded my best thinking. I couldn't fully process the end of that love while trying to remember why I believed in myself enough to start something new.

The wars and the peaces piled on top of each other without asking. I kept waiting for one of them to pause so I could deal with the others in order. That pause never came.

What I learned — slowly, painfully, and then with something approaching grace — is that I was never meant to sequence them. I was meant to carry them together, each one teaching me something the others couldn't, until I was ready to lay down what needed to be laid down and pick up what only I could carry forward. That is what this book was born from. Not from having the answers — but from having lived inside the questions long enough to trust them.

When Avoiding War Becomes Its Own Violence

There are times when refusing to fight is itself a form of harm. Staying silent when someone is being mistreated is not peace — it is agreement disguised as neutrality. Refusing to confront a partner's destructive behavior is not grace — it is consent. None of this requires you to stop caring about the person. It requires you to care about what is happening more than you care about avoiding the discomfort of naming it. And minimizing your own pain so others stay comfortable? Your body has another name for that. It's been using it for years.

You may have been raised to believe that good people don't fight. That conflict means failure. That if you were more patient, more spiritual, more loving, you would not feel this much anger. So you swallow your outrage until it turns into depression or apathy.

This season invites a different story: your anger may be the part of you that refuses to keep pretending everything is fine when it is not. The Stoics called this 'thumos' — the spirited part of the soul that rises against injustice not from hatred but from an inner sense of what ought to be. It is not your enemy. It is your most honest faculty.

The moment you stop resisting that anger and start listening to it, you realize it has been trying to recruit you into a necessary war—not against people's humanity, but against the patterns that are killing your joy, your trust, and your sense of self.

What Peace Really Means

Peace has one definition that holds across every context: the absence of ongoing harm. Everything else — quiet, calm, surface harmony — is just furniture arrangement.

False peace asks you to stay quiet so that nothing looks messy. It demands that you under-react, under-feel, and under-express so everyone else can stay comfortable. It promises harmony while silently requiring your disappearance. When you live in false peace, the truth finds other exits — through anxiety, resentment, numbness, or the sudden eruptions you can't quite explain even to yourself.

True peace is what happens after the right wars have been fought. It is the deep exhale that follows a hard conversation you needed to have years ago. It is the relief of walking out of an environment that has been slowly shrinking you. It is the quiet that comes after you stop trying to fix what will not heal.

True peace sometimes looks, from the outside, like you are starting conflict, bringing up the hard topic, naming the elephant in the room, saying, "this has to change." But inside, you know that the only path to genuine peace runs directly through this temporary storm.

The Quechua people of the Andes speak of 'pachakuti' — a turning of the world, a disruption that rights what has been upside down. What looks like a storm from inside it is often, from further out, the beginning of order being restored.

The Sacred Art of Strategic Peace

Not every tension requires a battle. Some differences are not injustices—they are just differences. Some disappointments are not betrayals—they are human limits. Some situations will not change no matter how much pressure you apply, and the war you keep waging is costing you more life than it could ever save.

There are several kinds of conscious peace worth knowing.

Restoration peace is ending conflicts that have become mutually destructive, recognizing when the battle itself has become the problem. The divorce that needs to stop being a war. The family feud that's poisoning generations. The internal battle against aspects of yourself that need acceptance, not conquest.

Strategic peace is recognizing when fighting wastes resources better used elsewhere. Not arguing with people committed to misunderstanding you. Not defending yourself against projections. Not engaging with bad-faith actors. This peace preserves your energy for battles that matter.

Protective peace is creating calm spaces where vulnerability can exist—the home that's a sanctuary, the relationship where you don't have to armor up, the internal quiet where creativity can emerge. This peace is an active creation, not a passive absence.

Surrender peace is accepting what cannot be changed through force—death, others' choices, natural consequences, the flow of life that moves regardless of your resistance. This is the hardest peace for fighters to make: the recognition that some forces are larger than individual will.

The Japanese concept of 'mono no aware' — the bittersweet awareness of impermanence — holds that the deepest peace is not the elimination of loss but the graceful acknowledgment of it. Some fights end not in victory but in understanding.

Laying down your weapons is how a fighter conserves what the next real battle will require. It is not a retreat. It is preparation. Peace asks: "Is this fight still connected to my values, my calling, my genuine responsibility—or am I just afraid of what it will mean if I stop swinging?" The people who fight well over a lifetime are not the ones with the most energy. They are the ones who know exactly what they are fighting for — and that knowledge tells them when to stop.

What you're building in this season is **emotional resilience** — not the ability to feel nothing in the hard moments, but the capacity to return to yourself after the fight, to rest without guilt during the peace, and to re-enter the next battle without the previous one still living in your body. Resilience is often misunderstood as toughness. It is elasticity — the ability to be moved, even shaken, without being permanently deformed. The person who never breaks down does not show resilience and shows numbness.

Resilience requires that something in you is still capable of being affected. The emotionally resilient person is not the one who never breaks down; they are the one who knows where to take the breakdown, how long to stay there, and how to come back with their integrity intact. This season asks you to be honest about what restores you — not what looks like rest from the outside, not what you think should be enough, but what genuinely returns you to yourself after you've given what the fight required.

If you only remember one thing from this season: War and peace are not enemies, they are tools. The question is never "Am I a peaceful person or a fighter?" It's "Am I fighting the right battles and resting in the right places?" Fight only where love requires it. Rest only where peace is honest. That is the whole season in two sentences.

Season Practice: Your War & Peace Map

Name Your Season

Draw two columns on a blank page.

Where I'm at War (conflicts actively engaged, places I feel defensive, resentful, or combative):

1.

2.

3.

Where I'm Keeping the Peace (situations I'm avoiding, places I say "it's fine" but my body tightens):

1.

2.

3.

Notice Your Mind

For each item in both columns, ask: "If I keep doing exactly what I'm doing here for another year, what will it cost me?" Write the honest answer next to each one. Don't soften it.

Notice Your Body

Pick one item from your war column and one from your peace
column. For each one, ask: "Is this a place where I need to enter the
fight—speak, act, set a boundary? Or is this a place where I need to
seek real peace—release, accept, or walk away?" Notice what your body
does with each question. Tightening usually means unfinished
business. Relief usually means you already know the answer.

One Aligned Action This Week

Choose one concrete step, either a small, strategic act of war or a small
act of genuine peace:

Act of war: One honest conversation you've been postponing. One
boundary you've been too tired to enforce. One decision you have
been delaying because it requires you to stop pretending.

Act of peace: Letting go of one fight that no longer serves you.
Stepping back from one conflict that was never your assignment.
Accepting one truth you've been arguing with because surrender feels
too much like defeat.

Battle and Truce Questions:
The Strategic Wisdom of Your Heart

Where are you currently fighting the wrong enemy—displacing your real conflict onto something or someone safer? What would it look like to turn and face the actual battle?

Where have you been calling avoidance "keeping the peace"? What is the honest name for what you're really doing there—and what would one act of genuine peace cost you?

Season Summary

> Most of us get war and peace backwards, we fight where peace would serve us and make peace where we should be at war.
> War, in this season, is any intentional move to stop harm when kindness and accommodation have already failed.
> Some battles are yours alone to fight. Some require partnership. Some were never yours at all—and fighting them is avoidance in disguise.
> Refusing to fight when fighting is needed is not peace. It is an agreement disguised as neutrality.
> False peace demands your disappearance. True peace is the exhale that follows the right fight finally fought.
> Strategic peace is not passivity—it is the wisdom to know when engaging wastes more than it gains.
> Surrender peace is accepting what cannot be changed by force—and redirecting your strength to what can.
> War and peace are not enemies. They are tools. The question is whether you're using them on purpose.
> The question is never whether you are a peaceful person or a fighter — it is whether you are fighting the right battles and resting in the right places.

Season Twelve:
A Time to Embrace,
A Time to Refrain from Embracing

There are seasons when your biggest problem is not that you don't care enough, it's that your care is scattered everywhere and anchored nowhere. You hug people you don't really trust. You share your soul with people who haven't earned it. You answer late-night calls from numbers that only dial when they're in crisis. Meanwhile, the people who could hold you well get the leftovers of your energy, your time, and your honesty. You have been generous with almost everyone except the people who deserved it most — and somehow that never made anyone's life better, including yours.

In other seasons, you swing the other way. You keep everyone at arm's length, including the ones who have proven themselves. You shrug off compliments, deflect concern, and change the subject when someone asks how you really are. You have relationships, but few safe embraces. You have contact, but not contact that lands.

This is the season where you decide who gets to touch your life—and how closely. Embrace is any way you let someone in: physically, emotionally, mentally, spiritually. Refraining is how you protect what is sacred in you from what cannot hold it or will never hold it at all. This season asks one simple, unnerving question: Who, exactly, has access to you—and have they earned it?

The Hug That Felt Like Betrayal

Maya's father had a gift—for other people's children. At church and in the neighborhood, he was a legend: warm, funny, always ready with a hug or an encouraging word. At home, he was mostly absent. When he did show up, his hugs were quick and perfunctory, followed by criticism disguised as concern.

When Maya was seven, she stopped running to him at the door. She learned to brace instead—to stiffen her shoulders, to smile politely, to let herself be held without really letting herself be touched. By thirty-three, she had a long list of people who could hug her body but had never met her heart. She dated people who adored being close to her, but when they held her, she felt like she was betraying something quiet and small inside that whispered: *"We don't feel safe."*

The Swahili concept of 'heshima' — dignity that must be actively protected, not just assumed — holds that some forms of closeness, offered without truth, are not kindness. They are a different kind of harm.

When her father became ill, everyone around her had the same script: *"Go sit by his bed." "Hold his hand." "You'll regret it if you don't."* The day she finally sat in the hospital room, he reached out for a hug. Her muscles did what they had always done, they moved on autopilot toward him.

Then something new happened. Her body locked. Not out of cruelty, but clarity. It was as if her nervous system said: *"No. Not like this. Not without the apology that never came. Not with everyone else in the room pretending there was never any distance at all."*

She panicked. *"What's wrong with me?"* she asked later. *"He's dying. Why couldn't I just give him what he wanted?"*

Her body refused to perform intimacy that had never actually been built. That refusal was not cold. It was the most honest thing in the room. Sometimes your refusal to embrace is not hard. It is honesty.

What Embrace Really Is

We tend to think of embrace as a physical act—but in this season, the lens is much wider. Embrace is any way you let someone close enough to leave fingerprints on your life.

Physical embrace is touch, proximity, letting someone into your space.

Emotional embrace is sharing your stories, your fears, your grief—letting someone see you cry, letting their care reach you.

Mental embrace is taking their perspective seriously, letting their ideas influence yours, and inviting their counsel into important decisions.

Spiritual embrace is sharing practices and letting someone's faith or worldview get closer to your deepest questions.

Energetic embrace is giving someone your full presence, letting their mood impact yours, adjusting your day around their needs.

You can withhold physical affection but give a massive emotional embrace—texting someone through every crisis while never letting them into your actual home. You can share a bed with someone while your heart remains bolted shut. Embrace is more complex, more layered, and far more expensive than we usually admit.

Ecclesiastes names it without ceremony: a time to embrace and a time to refrain from embracing. The wisdom was never in choosing one permanently — it was in developing the discernment to know which moment you were standing in.

This season invites you to stop treating embrace as a default setting and start treating it as a sacred allocation of your limited capacity.

How You Learned to Embrace—or Not

Your current patterns around closeness and distance didn't appear out of nowhere. They were formed in the emotional climate of your first relationships.

If love in your childhood felt like an invasion—no privacy, no boundaries, constant monitoring, you may now equate closeness with disappearance. Any request for a deeper connection feels like a demand to dissolve. You might shut down when someone wants to talk about feelings, joke your way out of serious conversations, or avoid being held unless you're in control of the timing and the exit.

If love felt like absence—emotional neglect, silence, no one noticing your inner world, you may now equate any attention with salvation. You might overshare quickly with anyone who seems interested, say yes to touch or closeness you don't really want because it feels better than emptiness, or stay in draining friendships because at least someone is there.

If love felt conditional—affection when you performed, distance when you failed—you may now treat every embrace as a test you must pass. You might work hard to be low maintenance so people don't leave, hide your needs until you explode, and then shame yourself for being too much, or over-function in relationships just to keep people close. Season Twelve is not here to blame your past. It's here to show you why your present feels the way it does. You are not broken. You are patterned. And patterns can be rewritten.

The Persian poet Rumi wrote: 'Out beyond ideas of wrongdoing and right doing, there is a field. I'll meet you there.' This season is that field — not a courtroom where your past is prosecuted, but an open space where your patterns can finally be examined without a verdict.

Most people spend years wondering why the same relational dynamic keeps finding them. The answer is almost always in one of these three rooms. Recognizing which one shaped you doesn't excuse the pattern — it gives you the address so you can finally go work on it.

Refraining: Not Rejection, but Right-Sizing

We misunderstand what it means to refrain from embracing. We treat every hesitation as unkind, every boundary as a wall, every "not that close" as a failure of love.

Refraining has one job: matching the level of access you grant someone to the level of safety they've demonstrated. Nothing more, nothing less, and nothing personal.

You refrain when someone has a long history of minimizing your pain, so you stop inviting them into your most tender stories. When a coworker consistently gossips about you, you stop sharing your personal life with them. When a family member uses your vulnerabilities against you, you keep the conversation at the surface and leave when they push for more. When a new person wants to move to instant best-friend status, you slow the pace instead of letting their urgency dictate your openness.

Refraining can look like short visits instead of long stays, group settings instead of one-on-ones, polite warmth instead of deep disclosure. It can sound like: "I care about you, but I'm not available for that level of access." Or simply: "I'm not comfortable going there with you."
You are not required to give someone more of yourself than their past behavior can safely hold.

Sometimes the person you most need to refrain from over-embracing is a past version of yourself — the one who needed chaos to feel alive or needed to be needed to feel worthy.

The Quiet Cost of Saying Yes to Everyone

Think of your capacity for intimacy like a house with a finite number of rooms. Every person you let in takes up space—some a corner, some a whole floor. You cannot invite everyone to move in and still have room to breathe.

When you say yes to everyone, you pay hidden costs. You answer late-night calls from people who only dial when they're in chaos, and then have no energy left for the friend who would have nourished you. You give emotional caretaking to relatives who refuse to do their own work and then feel strangely numb with the partner who genuinely wants to know you. You let exes and almost-relationships linger in your mind and wonder why you feel unavailable when someone honest shows up.

There is a reason you feel emotionally depleted even when you haven't been physically around many people. Embrace is expensive. Every conversation, every late-night DM, every *"Can I just vent?"* is a withdrawal from your account. Caring deeply about people is not the problem. The problem is when you care for others in ways that cost you the capacity to care at all.

The Ubuntu philosophy of southern Africa holds that 'I am because we are' — but it never argued that you must pour yourself empty to prove it. Community requires presence. Presence requires that something of you remains.

This season teaches you to stop handing out keys to your house just because someone is standing on the porch asking nicely—or pounding on the door demanding entrance.

The Art of Calibrated Closeness

Instead of thinking in binaries, either you let someone all the way in or you shut them out completely—this season invites you into calibrated closeness. Imagine a series of concentric circles around your life.

In the outer circles, there are acquaintances and loose connections. They get politeness, kindness, and basic respect. They do not get your secrets, your late-night availability, or your constant emotional labor.

In the middle circles are friends, colleagues, and community members you trust to varying degrees. They get selective sharing, some access to your inner world, a portion of your time, and support.
In the inner circle there are very few people. They get the full you—messy, glorious, unedited. They get your tears, your honest fears, your weirdness, your joy.

The Celtic tradition of 'anam cara' — soul friendship — held that there were perhaps one or two people in a lifetime with whom you could share the undefended truth of who you were. Not ten. Not twenty. One or two, chosen with great care and tended with great faithfulness.

Calibrated closeness means you stop dragging outer-circle people into your inner circle just because they're available or intense. The ability to read what a relationship can hold — not what you wish it could hold, not what it used to hold — is one of the most quietly sophisticated things a person can develop. You stop treating inner-circle people like they're in the outer ring, starving the relationships that deserve more of you. And you allow people to move both ways—deeper in as they prove themselves safe over time, and further out if they repeatedly show they can't handle the access they have.

Trust is not a light switch. It is a dial. The people who understand that — who let closeness deepen at the pace evidence supports — tend to build the most durable connections of their lives.

This is not cold. It is accurate. It's how you stop living at the mercy of other people's neediness or charisma and start living from the truth of what each connection can hold.

What you're building in this season is **emotional boundaries** — not walls, not cold distance, but an accurate internal map of how much of yourself each relationship can safely hold. An emotional boundary is a realistic assessment of what a particular connection can support without requiring you to disappear inside it. It is a realistic assessment of what a particular connection can support without requiring you to disappear into it. Most people have either never drawn this map or have drawn it according to guilt, history, and other people's expectations rather than actual demonstrated evidence of safety and mutuality.

Emotional boundaries ask a simple, difficult question of every relationship in your life: does this person's access to me match the level of care they have consistently shown? Where the answer is no in either direction, there is too much access, or not enough — this season is where you begin the slow, courageous work of recalibration.

When Embrace Heals You

Not all embrace is risky. Some of it is medicine.

There are people who, when they hold you, your shoulders drop three inches because your body recognizes: *"Safe."* There are conversations where you share something you were sure would scare someone away—and instead of backing up, they lean in. There are moments when you finally admit *"I'm not okay"* and someone says, *"I'm here,"* and something in you registers a kind of contact you forgot was possible.

Letting yourself receive that is also part of this season's work. For some people, this is the harder half. It may feel easier to set boundaries than to be held. You can control distance. You cannot fully control what happens once you open your arms.

So, this season asks: Can you let yourself be embraced where it is safe? Can you let in people who have proven themselves consistent, kind, and honest? Can you stop sabotaging the intimacy that is trying to heal you, because past intimacy wounded you? For many people, the most terrifying moment in any relationship is not conflict — it is being truly seen by someone who chooses to stay anyway.

When Refraining Saves You

On the other hand, there are people and patterns you simply cannot safely embrace—not now, maybe not ever.

The ex who only reaches out when their life falls apart, never when yours does. The family member who treats your vulnerability like ammunition. The friend who wants access to your time and energy but never shows up in your hour of need. The person whose closeness triggers shame or collapse in your body, no matter how good the story about them sounds.

Refraining here is refusing to sacrifice your soul on the altar of appearances — and that refusal is one of the most loving things you can do for yourself. It says: "I can love you as a human being without giving you unguarded access to the person you actually are."

In some cases, refraining may mean permanent distance. In others, it may mean provisional space: "Until you seek help. Until there's a pattern of change. Until you take responsibility for your part, I will not step closer."

The Confucian concept of 'zhengming' — the rectification of names, calling things what they actually are — reminds us that provisional distance is not cruelty. It is accuracy. You are simply naming the relationship as it exists rather than as you wish it did.

You are allowed to wait for fruit, not just apologies. You are allowed to let actions, not promises, determine the level of embrace.

The Shift: From Default Open to Discerned Welcome

The core shift of Season Twelve is moving from automatic availability to chosen intimacy. You stop treating your openness as something everyone is entitled to and start treating it as one of the most precious things you have to offer—which means you offer it where it will be honored.

Your mind will say: "If I don't let them in, I'm being cold." "If I stop being everyone's safe space, I'll end up alone." "If I let someone truly see me, they'll leave."

Your heart, underneath, already knows: real love does not demand that you abandon yourself to prove it. Some people will only stay as long as you ignore your own needs—and that is not love, it is dependency. The ones who are meant to be close will not be scared off by your humanity. They may actually be waiting for you to put your armor down.

Your openness is one of the most precious things you carry. Your distance, when chosen wisely, is how you make sure it stays that way. Your "no" to unsafe embrace is as holy as your yes to the arms that can actually hold you.

If you only remember one thing from this season: You were never meant to be everyone's safe place. The quality of your embrace matters more than its quantity. Recalibrating who gets access to you is not becoming colder—it is becoming clearer. And in that clarity, you finally have something real to offer the few people who have genuinely earned it.

Season Practice: The Access Audit

Name Your Season

Draw three concentric circles. Fill them honestly with names—not where you think people *should* be, but where they actually live in your daily life and heart.

- Inner circle (the full me—messy, honest, unedited).
- Middle circle (selective trust, portions of my time and inner world).
- Outer circle (politeness, kindness, basic respect—nothing more).

Notice Your Mind

For each person in your inner circle, ask these three questions and write your honest answers:

- Do I feel more myself or less myself after time with this person?
- Do they handle my vulnerability with care—or with dismissal, advice, or gossip?
- Is our closeness mutual, or do I carry most of the emotional load?

If someone consistently leaves you smaller, unseen, or over-responsible, they may need to move a ring out—not because they're bad, but because the access they have is injuring you.

Notice Your Body

Think of one person you've been giving inner-circle access to who may not have earned it. Does your body brace slightly before you see them — a kind of low-level preparation for impact? Now think of one person you've been keeping at distance who has consistently proven safe. Does something in you lean toward them when you imagine letting them one layer closer? Those responses are not accidents.

One Aligned Action This Week

Choose one boundary and one opening:

One boundary: A small, concrete way of refraining where you've been over-embracing. "I won't respond to texts after 9 p.m." Or: "I won't discuss my most tender struggles with people who haven't shown they can hold them."

One opening: A small, concrete way of embracing where you've been overly guarded. "I'll tell this friend what I'm really struggling with." Or: "I'll let myself be held without immediately making a joke or changing the subject."

Write both down. Expect discomfort on both sides. That discomfort is not proof you're wrong; it is proof you're living differently than your old patterns did.

Open Arms and Wise Walls Questions

Who in your life currently has inner-circle access that they haven't earned? What would it look like to quietly and compassionately move that relationship to a more honest level of closeness?

Who has earned more of you than you've been willing to give? What would one small act of genuine embrace—one moment of letting them actually in—look like this week?

Season Summary

> Your biggest problem may not be that you don't care enough—it's that your care is scattered everywhere and anchored nowhere.
> Embrace is more than physical touch—it's any way you let someone close enough to leave fingerprints on your life.
> Your patterns around closeness and distance were formed before you had a choice. You are not broken. You are patterned. And patterns can be rewritten.
> Your capacity for intimacy is finite. Every embrace costs something. Stop handing out keys just because someone is standing on the porch asking nicely.
> Calibrated closeness means letting people move both ways— deeper in as they prove themselves safe, and further out when they repeatedly show they can't handle what they have.
> Some embrace is medicine. Let yourself receive it where it is genuinely safe.
> You are allowed to wait for fruit, not just apologies. Let actions, not promises, determine the level of access.
> Your openness is a gift, not a requirement. Your distance is wisdom, not a defect.
> This season is not about becoming colder. It is about finally turning toward yourself with the kind of embrace you've spent years giving away—honest, discerning, fiercely protective, and unashamedly kind.

MOVEMENT FIVE: INTEGRATION
Living the Language You've Learned

By the time you reach this Movement, something has shifted. You have not just read about seasons. You have walked through them. You have let things die so other things could be born. You have uprooted what was draining you and planted what deserved a chance to grow. You have done the harder work of killing patterns that were killing you and healing wounds that were ready to close. You have become more honest with your own inner weather — allowing tears and laughter, mourning and dancing, clearing and gathering, tearing and mending. And you have brought all of that into the most complicated terrain of all: other people. You have practiced discernment with your words, your love, your fights, and your embrace. And somewhere in the middle of all of that, something in you quietly changed.

Now comes the question that every season has been quietly preparing you for: What does it look like to live this — not as a framework you consult, but as a language you speak?

Why This Movement Exists

There is a gap that nobody talks about in personal growth work. It sits between *understanding* something and *inhabiting* it. You can read every chapter, complete every practice, and still find yourself, under pressure, defaulting to the old patterns — shutting down when you should speak, fighting battles that aren't yours, embracing people who have never earned it, withholding yourself from people who have. Every tradition that has ever taken human transformation seriously has known this gap exists. The Zen masters called it the distance between 'knowing the path and walking the path.' The contemplative traditions called it the difference between intellectual conversion and heart conversion. Every serious spiritual practice in history has been designed for this gap.

That gap does not mean the work failed. It means you are a human being, not a software update. Change is not installed in a single session. It is practiced — awkwardly, imperfectly, and over time — until it becomes less a thing you do and more a way you move.

Movement Five exists for that gap. It is not a new set of concepts. It is the space where everything you've learned stops being information and starts becoming formation. Formation is slower than information. It happens in the repeated small choices, not the dramatic ones. It happens in what you do the second time a familiar season arrives — when you recognize the terrain and choose differently than you did before.

What Makes Integration Different

Ecclesiastes closes not with a neat resolution but with a summons: 'Fear God and keep his commandments, for this is the whole duty of man.' Whatever your relationship with that language, the underlying wisdom is consistent with every tradition that has ever thought seriously about human wholeness: at some point, you stop analyzing your life and start living it with full accountability.

Every previous Movement asked you to work on a specific domain: your foundations, your protection, your emotional life, your relationships. Each had its own seasons, its own patterns, its own practices.

Movement Five asks something different. It asks you to zoom out and look at your whole life at once — to see the multiple seasons running simultaneously across different areas, to stop demanding that life arrive in tidy, single-chapter installments, and to become the kind of person who can hold complexity without collapsing into it.
This is not easier than the earlier work. In some ways it is harder — because it requires you to give up the last quiet hope that if you just do enough inner work, life will eventually become simple.
Life will not become simple. But you can become wiser.

What's Ahead

Season Thirteen is the only season in this Movement — and deliberately so. It does not introduce a new pairing from Ecclesiastes. Instead, it honors what the Teacher of Ecclesiastes knew all along: that the seasons do not come one at a time. They overlap, collide, and layer on top of each other in ways that resist any tidy framework. The Teacher of Ecclesiastes knew this. The book does not end with a season. It ends with a recognition: that all of it — the dying and the living, the planting and the uprooting, the war and the peace — is part of one continuous, unrepeatable human life.

Season Thirteen is where you learn to live inside that reality without being undone by it. You will meet a familiar figure — Marco — at a very different point in his story than where you first found him. You will receive the central question that every season in this book has been pointing toward. And you will leave not with a finished version of yourself, but with something more honest and more durable: a way of reading your own life that will serve you through every season still to come.

The work you've done has not been wasted. It has been building a language.

Now you get to speak it.

Season Thirteen:
When All Season Converge

Right now, as you sit with these words, your life is not in one season. It has never been.

Something in you is being born. Something in you is dying. Something is just beginning to sprout. Something else is wildly overgrown and long overdue for uprooting. There is a part of you that is still fighting, another that is finally resting, another that is just now daring to hope. If you've ever thought, "Why am I so all over the place?" or "Why can't I just be in one clear chapter of life?" This is the season that answers you: because real life is not a single season. It is a climate. Many seasons layered on top of one another, all running at once. Season Thirteen is the moment you stop trying to untangle them perfectly and start learning to live wisely with all of them at the same time. This is where everything you've learned becomes less of a framework you remember and more of a language you speak without thinking.

Ecclesiastes knew this when it named not one season but fourteen — a full recognition that the complexity of a human life cannot be reduced to a single weather report or a single emotional chapter.

Marco's Second Waiting Room

A year after Marco sat with me holding divorce papers in one hand and a graduate school acceptance letter in the other, we found ourselves in a very different room. This time it was a hospital. His father had just had a stroke.

He looked older — not in a sad way, more in a "life has actually been lived" kind of way. The graduate program was in full swing. He was dating someone new who really listened. He had a healthier relationship with his ex-wife than he'd ever had while they were married. His kids were adjusting.

"What season are you in?" I asked, partly as a check-in, partly out of habit. He laughed. *"I have no idea. I think... all of them?"*

We started listing. In his career, he was in spring — new beginnings, a new identity as a student again. In his marriage, he was letting go of what they thought they were, gathering what remained true in autumn. In his relationship with his kids, a confusing mix of summer and winter — some days full of connection, other days frozen. In his relationship with his father, sudden winter — facing mortality, unfinished conversations, the shock of *"this might really end."*

He shook his head. *"If you looked at my life from the outside, you might say 'this is a season of...'"* He waved his hand, searching for the word. *"But from the inside?"* He looked up. *"It's all happening at the same time. There was no embarrassment in that admission anymore. Just recognition."*

Then he said something I'll never forget: *"Last year, this would have made me feel like a failure. Like, I was doing life wrong because it was so mixed. Now... it just feels like weather. I'm not panicking about every cloud anymore. I'm packing a jacket."*

That's Season Thirteen. The weather is still chaotic. But you are not.

The Life You Thought You'd Earn vs. the Life You Actually Have

Most of us were sold a subtle promise: if you do enough therapy, self-work, spiritual practice, and inner healing, you'll eventually arrive in a life where everything lines up. You imagined it — the stable relationship, the work that's meaningful, the body that's finally at peace, the past that's "processed," the future that's "aligned," the present that's "mindful."

In that fantasy, seasons still exist, but they arrive one at a time like polite guests, with clear beginnings and endings and plenty of emotional notice. You will move through them gracefully, like someone in a well-edited movie montage.

The life you have is different. Grief hits on the way to a promotion. Anxiety comes back right as you start to feel confident. A friendship ends the same month and a new love begins. The courage you gained in one area vanishes in another. You feel both grateful and resentful, both hopeful and scared, both alive and exhausted — sometimes before you finish your morning coffee.

This is exactly how a fully human life feels from the inside. Chaos is not the diagnosis. It is evidence that you are actually living one.

The goal was never to graduate into a seasonless existence. The goal was to become the kind of person who can look at their own complexity and say, "Of course. This makes sense," instead of "What's wrong with me?"

You Are Not Behind. You Are Multilingual.

By now, you've learned how beginnings and endings dance. When to plant and when to uproot. When to kill what is killing you and when to heal. When to break structures down and when to build new ones. How to weep and laugh without apologizing. How to mourn with others and dance without shame. How to throw away stones and gather what truly matters. How to tear illusions and sew real repair. When silence is protection and when speech is medicine. How to aim your love and your hate. How to choose your wars and your peace. Who to embrace and who to keep at a sacred distance.
You have not mastered these once and for all. You have learned their languages.

The ancient Egyptians called this 'sia' — the divine faculty of perception, the ability to read the hidden order beneath the surface of things. What you've been building across these seasons is a version of that: the capacity to read your own life accurately enough to respond to what is there.

Season Thirteen is not a new season with brand-new rules. It is the realization that you are now multilingual in your own life. You can notice a relational pattern and say, "This is a time to uproot, not invest more. That ability to step back from your own experience and read it accurately — to be both inside the feeling and slightly above it at the same time — is what separates reaction from response across an entire lifetime. You can sit in grief and know "This is weeping, not weakness." You can feel anger rise and recognize "This is a holy war, not me overreacting again" or "This is an old fight I don't need to fight anymore." You can feel the pull to say yes and gently reply This is a time to refrain from embracing. My energy is not infinite.

You are no longer stuck with one default response. You have a whole vocabulary of wise responses to choose from, depending on the season.

You are not behind. You are becoming fluent.

Across all the seasons, you have been building emotional capacities — acceptance, discernment, courage, flexibility, authenticity, integration, clarity, honesty, voice, aim, resilience, and boundaries. Season Thirteen is what it looks like when all of them are present at once, moving together, serving a life you've chosen to live on purpose.

The Myth of the Final Season

Let's clear up one last quiet lie: there is no graduation season where everything stays resolved. There is no permanent summer of emotional enlightenment.

If you expect that, you will misinterpret every new winter as failure, every new conflict as proof you've regressed, every new grief as a sign you didn't heal right the first time.

Season Thirteen invites you to accept a different reality. You will have more beginnings. You will face more endings. You will plant again, uproot again. You will love again, hate what harms again. You will fight again, make peace again. You will embrace again, refrain again. The difference is this: the next time these seasons come, you will not meet them as a beginner.

The Zen tradition speaks of 'shugyo' — a lifelong commitment to deepening practice, not a curriculum you complete. Mastery is not a destination. It is a direction.

You might still feel afraid — but you will recognize the terrain. You will think: "Ah. I know this winter. I've met it before. I know how to make soup this time. I know who to call. I know how not to rip up my own roots just because I'm cold."

Life does not promise fewer seasons. It offers you the chance to become less afraid of them.

What you're building in this season — and what all twelve previous seasons have been quietly constructing together — is **emotional maturity**. Emotional maturity looks like holding complexity without demanding that it simplify before you act. It includes fear, reactivity, and old patterns — but it no longer lets them drive. Emotional maturity is the ability to hold complexity without demanding that it simplify before you act. It is the capacity to be in grief and still show up for work, to be uncertain about a relationship and still make a decision, to be in winter in one area of your life and in spring in another — and not treat that coexistence as evidence that something is wrong with you.

Emotionally mature people are not people who have stopped feeling. They are people who have learned to feel accurately, respond wisely, and keep moving through seasons they cannot control — because they have finally stopped confusing the weather with their worth.

The You Who Survived Every Season

Pause for a moment and look back — not just at the pages of this book, but at the pages of your own life.

There was a time when you did not know any of this language. You just survived. You invented the languages of survival before anyone taught you the languages of wisdom: the careful management of other people's emotions, the exhausting performance of being fine, the slow disappearing act you called being easy to love.

Those strategies, for a while, worked. They got you through seasons you had no roadmap for. There is a version of you — maybe five, twelve, eighteen, thirty — who did the very best they could with what they knew.

Season Thirteen is where you stop looking back at those earlier versions of yourself with only criticism and start looking back with gratitude and grief. Gratitude, because they got you here. Grief, because they had to carry so much without the wisdom you are holding now.

You are not meant to wage war against your younger self. This is the season where you finally embrace them instead. You become the guide for them that they never had. When you feel yourself slipping into old patterns, instead of asking "What's wrong with you?" you can say: "Ah. I know who this is. This is the twelve-year-old who thought being quiet was the only way to stay safe. Let me sit with them. Let me show them the new options we have now."

The West African griot tradition understood this — that the keeper of stories is not just a historian but a healer, because naming what happened accurately is the first step toward not repeating it. You are becoming the griot of your own life.

You are not just learning to handle future seasons. You are redeeming the past ones.

Living With Multiple Forecasts at Once

How do you live when several seasons are active at the same time? Consider a day like this: you wake up grieving a loss. You go to a job that is growing. You come home to a relationship that is struggling. You are quietly working on a dream that no one sees yet. You are setting a boundary in a friendship for the first time.
No wonder one *"how are you?"* feels impossible to answer. The ability to hold multiple emotional truths at once — grieving and grateful, afraid and hopeful, finished and beginning — without demanding that one of them win is one of the quietest signs of genuine growth.

Instead of flattening your life into one word — *"good," "busy," "tired"*- Season Thirteen invites you to become specific with yourself, even if you can't explain it to everyone else. You might say in your journal or to one trusted friend: "In my work life, I'm in spring — lots of newness, lots of learning." "In my body, I feel like I'm in winter — it's tired, healing, slower than I want." "In my friendships, I'm in a mix of summer and autumn — some are rich, some are clearly fading." "In my inner world, I'm in construction — breaking things down and building new beliefs."

The Celtic concept of 'thin places', locations where the distance between what is and what could be becomes almost transparent, suggests that honest self-mapping creates its own kind of thin place. When you see your life clearly, the next step tends to reveal itself.

This kind of honest self-mapping can feel uncomfortable at first — not because it's hard to do, but because it removes your ability to keep pretending that one difficult area isn't affecting everything else.

A simple weekly practice: ask yourself what season you are in across four areas — your relationships, your work, your body and health, and your inner life. You don't need perfect answers. You just need honest ones.

Naming your seasons doesn't instantly fix them. But it aligns your expectations with reality — and that is where most of your unnecessary suffering has lived. You stop demanding harvest where you're in planting. You stop berating yourself for being sad in a place that's clearly in winter. You stop shaming yourself for feeling overwhelmed when you are, in fact, carrying three demanding seasons at once. And you start offering yourself the right kind of care for each area of your life.

The One Question That Changes How You Move

By now, you've heard this question in different forms throughout these chapters. Season Thirteen crystallizes it into its final, simplest form: "Given the season I'm actually in, what is the most loving next step I can take?"

Not 'What would finally prove I'm enough?' Not 'What would guarantee I never feel this way again?' Just: 'Given this season, what is the most loving, honest, sustainable next step?' Just: "Given this season of grief, what is the most loving next step I can take? Given this season of new beginnings, what is the most loving next step? Given this season of war, or of peace, of embrace, or of refraining — what is the most loving, honest, sustainable next step?"

The Sufi tradition holds that the highest intelligence is not knowing all the answers — it is knowing which question to ask when you are lost. This is that question.

The ability to ask a different question of each different season — rather than bringing the same answer to every circumstance — is the whole game. It is what every previous season in this book has been building toward.

Sometimes that step will be bold: the conversation, the boundary, the resignation, the move. Sometimes it will be gentle: a nap, a walk, a phone call, a journal entry, a decision to tell the truth to one safe person.

Season Thirteen is where you accept that you cannot control the timing of your seasons — but you can always choose your next step inside them.

Your Life as a Sacred Relay

Think of how you arrived at this moment. Somewhere in your history — your family line, your community, your culture — someone learned a hard lesson and passed it forward.

A grandparent finally said, *"The hitting stops with me."* A parent quietly started therapy even when nobody around them understood it. An older sibling began setting boundaries in a family that didn't know what that word meant. A friend modeled what mutual, healthy love could look like.

Their courage became your starting line. Their courage became the ground you were standing on before you even knew the ground existed. The deepest form of empathy is not feeling what someone else feels in the moment. It is having walked through enough seasons yourself that you can recognize theirs — and know, without having to be told, what kind of presence they need.

If you can't immediately name who that person is for you, consider that you may be the first in your line to walk this far. That is not a disadvantage. That is a different kind of courage.

Now, whether you like it or not, the way you navigate your seasons is becoming part of someone else's relay. A child, a friend, a sibling, a partner, a coworker, a stranger who is watching more closely than you know — you are giving them a live demonstration of what is possible in human life.

When you leave a job that was killing you without needing a scandal to justify it, you change what someone else believes is possible. When you apologize first in a conflict without losing your dignity. When you grieve openly without apologizing for it. When you ask for help before you collapse. When you embrace someone worthy, even though your past taught you to flinch. When you refrain from embracing someone who hasn't earned it, even though your culture calls you cold.

You are not just changing your life. You are quietly bending what someone else believes is possible for theirs.

Season Thirteen is where you realize: you are not just surviving seasons. You are redefining them for whoever comes after you.

The Aha You've Been Moving Toward

If there is one thing I hope stays with you long after these pages, it is this:

You were never the problem. The way you were fighting your seasons was.

You weren't broken for grieving long after other people moved on. You were in a different season. You weren't weak for needing rest. You were in winter while everyone around you was performing in summer. You were in winter while they were in summer. You weren't heartless for leaving a situation others could tolerate. Your season of war arrived earlier. You weren't needy for wanting closeness. You were in a season of embrace. You weren't cruel for setting distance. You were in a season of refraining that saved your life.

The person you've been calling your own worst enemy was often just someone trying to live a summer life in a winter season — trying to harvest in a field that needed to be uprooted first, trying to make permanent peace in a place that still needed a holy fight.

Once you see that, the case against yourself falls apart. Not because you've become perfect — but because you've finally understood what was happening. You can look at the next hard thing and think — not "What's wrong with me that this is happening?", but "What season is this? And what does this season need from me?"

That's not just a mindset. That's maturity.

Your Seasons Are Not Your Enemy

You began this book perhaps believing your life was a problem to be solved, a sequence of mistakes to be corrected, a series of delays to be overcome. I hope you end it seeing your life as a landscape to be walked with wisdom.

The seasons will keep changing. You will still have days that feel like contradictions, months that feel like whiplash, years that don't fit into any neat story you can tell at dinner. But you will never again be completely at the mercy of that chaos.

Because now, when the wind shifts, you can say: *"Ah. I know this. I've walked through this kind of weather before."* You may still be afraid — but you won't be confused about what's happening. You have names for things now. And a named thing can no longer pretend to be something it isn't.

Your seasons are not your enemy. They are the rhythm of a life fully lived. They are the way your soul, your relationships, your work, and your world move you into growth you would not choose on your own.

Respect every season, even the ones you'd never choose. They are not punishing you. They are preparing you. You can listen to them. You can stop fighting them long enough to ask: *"What are you here to teach me?"*

And when you do, you will discover something quietly miraculous: The only person who was ever truly in your way was also the one person who can walk you through every season you will ever face. *You.*

Not the shamed, panicked version of you who thought they had to control the weather — but the wiser, kinder version of you who knows how to read the sky, pack for the journey, ask for help when the storm hits, and keep walking anyway.

That is who you are becoming. That is who you already are, more than you realize.

You have walked through multiple kinds of seasons in these pages. The seasons will keep changing. You will not face them as the same person who first opened this book.

If you only remember one thing from this season — and from this entire book: You were never the problem. The way you were fighting your seasons was. Name the season you're in. Give it what it needs. Take the most loving next step you can. Then trust the process — because the process has been working on you all along.

Seasonal Practice: Your Season Inventory

Name Your Season

Once a week — or whenever life feels overwhelming — take five minutes to map where you actually are. Be honest, not aspirational. What season am I in right now across these four areas:

Relationships: ____

Work: ____

Body / Health: ____

Inner Life (thoughts, emotions, spirit): ________________________

Don't force one answer per category. You might be in spring and winter simultaneously in the same relationship. That's allowed. That's real.

Notice Your Mind

Look at what you wrote. Where are you demanding harvest in a field that's still in planting? Where are you shaming yourself for being in winter when winter is exactly what this place needs? Write down one place where your expectations are completely mismatched with the actual season you're in.

Notice Your Body

Pick the area of your life that feels heaviest right now. Where do you feel that weight in your body? Now ask yourself: "If I gave this area exactly what its season actually needs — not what I wish it needed, not what would look good, but what this season genuinely calls for — what would that feel like?" Notice where your body softens. That softening is pointing you home.

One Aligned Action This Week

Ask yourself: "Given the season I'm actually in right now, what is the most loving next step I can take?"

Write it down. Make it specific. Make it honest. Make it doable — not heroic, not impressive, not what you think you should be able to do. Just the truest, most loving next step.

Then take it.

Confluence:
Navigating the Waters Where All Your Seasons Meet

Look back at the version of you who picked up this book. What season were you in then that you didn't have language for? What would you say to that version of yourself now?

What is one pattern you used to call a personal failing that you can now recognize as a response to a season you didn't know how to read? How does naming it that way change how you feel about yourself?

Season Summary

> Real life is not a single season — it is a climate. Many seasons layered on top of each other, all running at once.
> The goal was never to graduate into a seasonless existence. The goal was to become someone who can look at their own complexity and say *"Of course. This makes sense."*
> You are not behind. You are becoming multilingual — fluent in the language of your own seasons.
> There is no final season where everything stays resolved. The difference is that next time the hard seasons come, you will not meet them as a beginner.
> Your younger self deserves gratitude, not only criticism. They got you here. You can be their guide now.
> Naming your seasons — across relationships, work, body, and inner life — aligns your expectations with reality. That is where most unnecessary suffering ends.
> The question that changes everything: "Given the season I'm actually in, what is the most loving next step I can take?"
> You are part of a sacred relay. The way you navigate your seasons is already becoming someone else's starting line.
> You were never the problem. The way you were fighting your seasons was.

The seasons will never stop and will always keep changing. You will not face them as the same person who first opened this book.

Before You Go

I wrote this book because I needed it.

My mother had died. A relationship I loved deeply was ending. A business I believed in was still too fragile to trust. Life handed all three to me at once and didn't wait for me to be ready. For a long time I thought the chaos meant something was wrong with me — that people who had done the work didn't end up carrying this much simultaneously. What I eventually discovered is that I wasn't failing. I was in multiple seasons at once and I had no language for any of them.

Language changed everything. Not the circumstances. Not the grief. Not the difficulty of the endings or the uncertainty of the beginnings. But the way I was standing inside all of it. Once I could name the season, I could stop fighting it long enough to hear what it was asking of me.

That's the only thing I wanted to give you. Not a map that removes the difficulty. Not a promise that enough inner work will eventually simplify your life. Just language. The kind that helps you look at what is happening and say: I know this. I know what this season needs.

You will face hard seasons after you close this book. Some you'll choose. Most of you won't. And in those moments — when life hands you two or three impossible things at once — I hope something from these pages surfaces quietly and says: this is not evidence that something is wrong with you. This is what a fully human life feels like from the inside.

You are not behind. You are not broken. You are in a season.
And now you have the language to say which one.
The seasons will keep changing.
So will you.
That is not a problem. That is the whole point.